OFF-RO
RACING
& PREPARATION

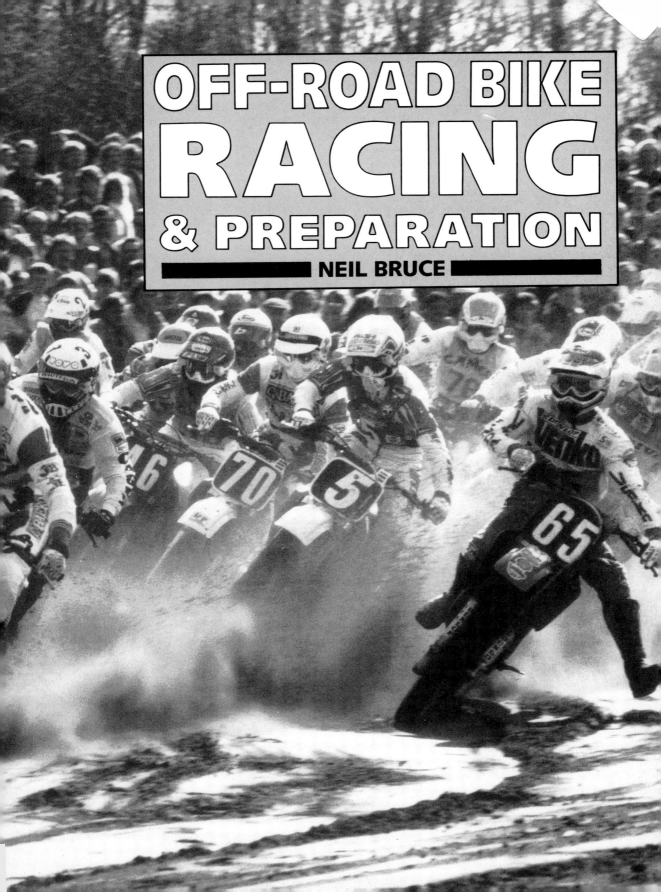

OFF-ROAD BIKE
RACING
& PREPARATION

NEIL BRUCE

Published in 1989 by Osprey Publishing
59 Grosvenor Street, London W1X 9DA

British Library Cataloguing in Publication Data

Bruce, Neil
    Off-road bike racing & preparation for motocross &
enduro.
    1. Racing motorcycles. Off-road racing
    I. Title
    796.7'5

ISBN 0-85045-889-7

Phototype set by Keyspools Ltd, Warrington

Printed in Great Britain by
Butler & Tanner Ltd, Frome and London

Contents

Foreword

by Roger Harvey

In my experience, there is no substitute for experience! But having said that, the process of learning to ride a motorcycle off-road is made easier, quicker and less painful if the techniques involved are explained in terms that can be easily understood. This book is unique in its method, by first describing in detail the main aspects of riding technique in words, and then illustrating each technique, step by step, in photographic sequences, so that the reader can see for himself exactly what is being described.

Good riding technique is essential to safe riding. A rider who has been taught to ride properly, will ride with greater control and therefore safety. With the feeling of safety and control comes confidence. With confidence, a rider will be able to go faster without having to compromise safety margins. Good technique also means safe technique, which in turn results in greater enjoyment of the sport.

I have been fortunate enough to have been closely involved with off-road motorcycle sport for more than 20 years — as a spectator, wild-riding junior, 'hot prospect', expert rider, world championship contender, British Champion, professional motocross coach and, lately, as team manager with Yamaha. I've had a lot out of the sport and a great deal of fun on the way.

No one ever stops gaining experience, even after their racing days are over. I hope that many riders will be able both to enjoy reading this book and then find they are able to benefit from my experience and the riding techniques offered within. Learn the techniques and then just keep on practising. Always try to remember — the reason you got a bike in the first place was to have FUN and don't forget that!

Safe riding.

Roger Harvey

Acknowledgements

A project like this would have been impossible without the help of a great many people. I would like to thank in particular Roger Harvey for his enthusiasm and expertise, Rob Herring, Warren Edwards and Ady Smith for their skill and patience, Steve Goodyear for his tips, Adam and Vic for their ability with the shutter, John, Tom and Olga Pugh for their hospitality and help with the enduro section (together with Arwyn and Clive), Tim Matthews for the use of his track, the AMCA for the use of Crick, and finally Martin Christie and Vic Barnes for their welcome advice.

Introduction

This book is aimed at *all* motocross and enduro riders. I hope that rank novices will find the techniques a useful starting point to refer to as they begin to learn how to handle a motorcycle off-road. The clubman standard riders, who can already ride their bike but are unable to always make it do quite what they want it to, should use this book a chapter at a time.

Read a particular section, say for instance, Berm Corners. Read it and look at the sequences in the photographs until you really understand in your own mind just what you ought to be doing, then go out and practise it until you can feel the difference in your riding technique. Pick on something you think you can do reasonably well, but accept there might be a better way of doing it. Check it out in the book. If a different technique is illustrated, see if it makes sense to you. If it does, give it a try. Use it as a reference book.

For all the experts and the 'gods' above them, you might even be in the book! Now that will make you read it, if nothing else will. If you really are a good rider, you will read to bolster your own confidence, to see whether you *are* in fact doing it all right and are just as stylish as you thought you were anyway, and for safety's sake—just in case Harvey has taken the mickey out of you in one of his anecdotes that pepper the motocross section.

Roger Harvey is renowned for his riding technique, built up over years of competing at the very highest levels in motocross circuits all over the world. He was Under-21 British Champion in 1971, has received caps for England at Motocross Des Nations in 125, 250 and 500 cc classes, has numerous international race wins under his belt, was fifth in the 1976 125 cc World Championship and was British 125 cc Champion in 1983. Roger's technique has always been built around safety. The proper way to ride a bike is also the safest way to ride.

Roger, aside from being responsible for Mitsui's off-road activities, is a qualified ACU instructor. He has been teaching all sorts of people how to ride at organized riding schools for a number of years and many of today's top riders owe at least some part of their skill to Roger's experience.

What is described in the motocross section of this book is what he has been teaching for years. What *we* have the opportunity to do in this book is to see major aspects of that same motocross technique illustrated, step by step in series of photographs. Motocross tracks have changed quite a bit over the past few years, (so the ever-green Roger assures me!) evolving into the more spectacular, supercross-type circuits in recent times. The technique explained here is a valid foundation for all aspects of motocross and can be adapted where necessary to suit an individual rider's style. In fact, enduro riders will probably benefit most from this book, as so much of the technique needed to compete successfully in enduros comes from motocross.

Remember, the best riders are always the safest ones, irrespective of experience. I hope you will all read this book primarily for enjoyment and then find you can practise and benefit from the individual techniques when you go out riding.

PART ONE

MOTOCROSS RIDING TECHNIQUE

1   Walking the track

2   First practice

3   Starting

4   First corner

5   Acceleration

6   Berm corners

7   Flat corners

8   Ramp jumps

9   Table-top jumps

10   Jumping

11   Braking and acceleration bumps

12   Whoops

13   Passing

14   Braking

15   Crashing

16   Play riding

1 Walking the track

An essential part of your pre-race preparation is the time-honoured pastime of 'walking the track'.

Organizers can, and frequently do, change the track layout. Even tracks you might have raced at many times before should be given the respect of a visual inspection before you even think about putting on a helmet. Apart from getting an idea of the track's layout, walking also gives you the chance to look for lines into and out of corners and surface changes. Always look forward, in the direction you will actually be racing. Look back down the track if you are struggling with a particular line or corner.

One of the benefits of walking the track is that you can have a good look out for some of those small things that might make a big difference if you hit them blind. Check for rocks that might be lurking under the surface, tree roots or stumps, odd-shaped bumps that could pitch you off if you don't hit them just right. Strange cambers take on a different perspective at walking pace, as do places where the track crosses older parts of track and you are likely to find ruts. These are all reasons why, provided you are serious about your racing, it is worthwhile taking the time to walk the track.

Sometimes even the pros have to compromise themselves though, as Roger found on one occasion in France.

'Following a race in England, I had to drive overnight to race the next day at Tibberville in France. Over there the starts are generally quite early. I arrived late and so found myself without the time to walk the track. Instead I decided to ride around the track just taking it easy. On the main straight, the rest of the guys were overtaking me going quite quickly. Suddenly, at the last minute I saw a ten-foot deep drainage ditch opening up in front of me. Fortunately, I was going so slowly that I just managed to stop in time. I had to ride back down the track to get sufficient speed up to clear it. The 6–7 ft gap was no problem at racing speed, but because I was going slowly I could have had a very nasty crash. . .'

Then there was the time Bob Wright found himself in a similar position.

'There was a French International event at Brou. Bob arrived quite late and didn't have a lot of chance to practise before the race. Anyway, he went out on the track and totally mixed up two different jumps that had similar approaches and take-offs. Unfortunately they had totally different landings. One landing was straight on, while the other was on a bend. Bob hit one thinking it was the other and took off, only to find himself soaring over the fence and crowd before landing in the in-field. The crowd loved it but Bob was left chasing around the in-field trying to find a way back on to the track. In fact, I don't think he ever managed to rejoin the race. . . !'

At Château de Loire, again in France, Roger found a unique but decidedly unorthodox way to ensure quick first aid. . .

'I was putting the track together at Château de Loire during the French 250 cc GP practice. There was this big, muddy hill. On the approach to the hill you had to go through a watersplash, which was in fact a brook, then a short, flat area before you started to climb the hill. Coming round this time I thought I would clear the hill easy if I could hit the first part, climbing out of the brook, hard enough. I got crossed up in two ruts coming out of the brook but thought to myself, no problem. As soon as I can get on to the little flat bit, it'll straighten out. I left it wound flat-out and attacked the hill.

'As I came out of the brook the bike gripped and hung a left, straight into some chestnut palings. This would not normally have presented a problem but the palings just folded down and turned into a perfect take-off ramp for me. I hit them and took off, finally landing smack in the middle of a ridge-type first aid tent which had been sitting well out of harm's way in the in-field. I hit it with the back wheel one side of the tent and the front wheel the other. The whole lot collapsed down around me!

'Perry Leask and Paul Hunt were standing nearby and they were just creased up laughing. The French first aid guy rushed up and grabbed me by the sleeve and said "Oiii, monsieur, ça va? Aaare you OK?"

"Yeah, I'm alright. . ." I replied ". . . but I'm really sorry about yer tent. . ."'

2   First practice

First practice should offer the rider a good chance to have a look at a track. Unfortunately, some meetings leave precious little time for practice. NEVER race around a track blind, not knowing what is coming up next. If there is not a lot of time put aside for practice then you must at least make the effort to get around the track and have a look to see what everyone else is doing, looking for one or two neat lines that you can keep to yourself and use later on in the day.

Provided you are allowed the proper time to practise, take it easy on the first couple of laps. Remember practice is what it says; it is *practice* and not a race. Next, start to piece the track together. Do one part of it fast, then back off. Relax, do another part fast and so on until you end up with lots of pieces that you have been over quite fast and you are happy with. If there is a section you are not happy with, watch how other riders tackle it or even follow some of them through it.

It might even pay you to walk certain parts after your practice to have another static look at a particular corner, or again, watch other riders. You should finish practice with a sound knowledge of the track and feeling confident about your ability to race over the entire course.

In the days when Harvey was a lad with high hopes but a runny nose and short trousers, he learnt from following older riders, but found as his career matured (and *he* too got older!) that the tables were turned. . . .

'When I was younger, I used to follow the more experienced riders who knew how to use the track properly to its best advantage. As I got older and subsequently more experienced, I noticed how I used to be left alone during practice until the last two or three laps. These were the ones I would normally try to put in quite quickly. Obviously, it pays to look over your shoulder to see who is following you in that situation. You don't want to be showing all your race-winning lines to your arch-rival, now do you?

As I looked over my shoulder to see who was following me, there would inevitably be two guys in particular, Kevin Froud and Mark Fulton, who had suddenly popped out of nowhere and were sitting, eager-eyed, on my tail, trying to see my lines. This often meant I couldn't put in my "quick laps" because of them sitting there, or alternatively I would show them some really silly, lousy or bum lines. . . !'

3   Starting

'The best starters are the ones who cheat the best. There are many different types of start; elastic, fold-down gate, up-and-away gate, T-bar. But basically, you have got to cheat like hell! That is what it's all about!' (Quote from a former British Motocross Champion who shall remain nameless.)

The start is the single most important part of the race. It is therefore essential to get it right. It is also essential to bend the rules, take any advantage you possibly can, look for that extra little edge, use acquired local knowledge, indulge in your fair share

of skulduggery or any other definition you care to use for a little harmless *cheating*.

Cheating has such an undignified, almost dirty ring to it! But anyone who doesn't cheat will simply never make the holeshot. And some elements of cheating at starts come down to merely using common sense.

With elastic starts, position yourself in the centre where the bikes are going to leave first, rather than at the edges. Always check out the starter at a previous race to yours. Does he have any particular mannerisms before he actually starts the race? For instance, does he look left, then right, then back to the

ABOVE

British Open Motocross Championship at
Torquay 1983. Guess which one's Harvey. The
best start position for the first corner was to the
left of the picture, where Thorpe (number 2 on his
helmet) and the rest are. During previous heats,
Roger had noticed that the gates fell first on the
far side, and you can see the result for yourselves
in this picture that he told Jack Burnicle
beforehand might be worth taking! (*Jack Burnicle*)

ABOVE RIGHT

At the old Newbury track, the best place to start
for a sweep into the first corner, was over to the
left. Roger Harvey always used to start over to the
right, either number 1 or 2 T-bar, because a rider
could hang his head over the fence and watch the
start pedal being pressed. With the concrete start
(now banned), you could get your wheel spinning,
time the start to perfection and go straight across
everyone as they swept into the corner. Roger has
utilized this technique to nab the holeshot here at
Newbury during the British Open Motocross
Championship in 1983 and is ahead of Thorpe—2
(Honda), Whatley—4 (Suzuki) and Hudson—1
(Yamaha) (*Jack Burnicle*)

centre before pressing the pedal? If that is his style, then when it comes to your start wait for him to glance to the left, then to the right, then you GO!

Be aware of the mechanics behind each starting method. Look for the first thing that will move and either drop your gate or give you that fraction of a second's anticipation over the guy beside you who might simply be looking at the top of his gate. On a T-bar, for example, a pin is pulled by a length of chain. Wind the chain up on your gate to take up any slack, while pulling your pin out as far as it will go without letting the gate drop. Then the first gate to drop should be yours.

Some riders have tried jumping the T-bar, making sure among other things that they don't catch their exhaust pipes on the edge of the gate. Find out what the penalties are for false starting; disqualification, relegation to the back, or even in some cases, making you start facing the wrong way round. Then you can weigh up the penalties against the possible chance of a flying start.

There is no point, for instance, in false starting in the heats. Wait for the final or the big money earner—then false start. If you end up in a live, televised race, then it is certainly worth trying for a flyer of a start. The organizers are unlikely to pull you all back and actually call a false start in front of millions of live viewers . . . are they?

Some starters can be 'helped along'. On a flag start, try the starter out as he looks down the line. As his eyes get to you, pop your clutch and shoot forward a bit, always remaining prepared to go. See how he reacts. If he panics enough to drop the flag and let the race go, then you can take over as starter for the day.

Other 'techniques' can be used to upset your fellow competitors while on the line. If you see someone gazing about on the line, try diving for your clutch as if you are going for a flyer, they might panic and false start. Or, perhaps you are all on the line, the start's been delayed, and in this particular case you are lined up beside the one guy you have to beat to win the championship and this is the decider. Finally you are all about to start. Tension mounts and nerves strain. As you bring your elbows up for the start itself, bang

ABOVE

One of Roger's old dodges to ensure he wasn't
crowded at the start was to bend over by his bike
while riders were assembling, pretending to be
checking his carburettor or fuel tap, until the
riders were in place around him. Once satisfied
that they were in their final positions, he would
get back on to his bike and prepare for the off
(*Vic Barnes*)

ABOVE AND BELOW RIGHT

You can adjust the slack on the chain and move
the pin as far as it will go, so that when the line of
starting gates gets pulled, yours should drop first!
(*Vic Barnes*)

his elbows with yours just as he's getting his act together. This might just break his concentration and then as he turns to take issue with you—the gate drops and away you go. . .

Some riders try another distracting or psyching-out method. Just as all heads are down and you are watching your gates, start shouting and making a commotion as if there is some sort of major problem, trying all the time to catch the attention of the riders immediately around you while keeping a wary eye on your gate. As it drops, away you go leaving them at the line looking at each other and wondering what on earth is going on.

In amongst all this messing about, there is also some riding technique useful to the game of starting. First of all, run through a mental checklist.

While at the line, take the bike out of gear and keep it in neutral. As late as possible, pull the clutch in with four fingers and select your gear: second gear for most sizes of bike but possibly third gear for 500s if it is wet. Just in case the bike has jumped out, check it is in gear by easing the clutch out until you can feel it biting, then pull it back in again with just two fingers, leaving two fingers wrapped around the handlebar. This way, when you fire the clutch you have a proper grip on the bars.

Make sure you are in the correct seated attack position with elbows up, head down over the steering head and sitting in the middle of the bike. Keep a constant throttle before the start. Keep it about a third open. Not having your arm go up and down on the throttle will help your concentration and avoid you bogging your engine by firing the clutch when the revs are going down instead of up!

Full commitment is needed at the start. No room for faint hearts here. Fire the clutch and keep the bike flat out, using as much throttle as possible depending on track conditions. One of the reasons it is worth practising starts is to let you assess the conditions and grip and adjust your starting procedure and positioning accordingly.

Gearchanges should be made under full power, making sure you always use the clutch by just feathering it. The next time you should shut off is for the first obstacle. If it is wet, sit further back. If it is concrete or a similar surface, sit back but come forward up the saddle as you get on to the grippier stuff. If the bike goes sideways or wheelies, control it with the clutch—do not shut off. Under no circumstances shut off before the first obstacle. Only if you are Rob Herring might you be inclined to shut

Before the actual start of a race, keep the bike in neutral until the last possible moment, then use all four fingers on the clutch and put the bike into gear (*Vic Barnes*)

Next, adopt the starting position with your weight in the middle of the bike, elbows up, head over the pivot point, with just two fingers on the clutch. Keep your throttle constant so that your arms will be in one position when you fire the clutch and go (*Vic Barnes*)

off sometime well after the first obstacle . . . the rest of us are mere mortals!

Remember—*full commitment*!

During a long and illustrious career as a professional rider, Roger Harvey learnt the importance of a 'good' start. Below are just a few of the many stories he disclosed to me that revolved around the noble (nobbled?) art of starting as recounted by the man himself.

'At one race a young lad was being allowed to do the starts by his father. The father was telling the son when to drop the flag, so I just sat there on the line watching the father and ignoring the son. Out of three of the four races, I was going like 20 yards up the track past the son, by the time the flag actually dropped. . . .

'One of the reasons I started checking the bike was in gear before the start resulted from experience with an old OSSA I used to race. The engine timing on it was so critical that if it was just slightly out and the revs were allowed to drop, the engine could switch from running forwards to running backwards and all this without the rider being aware of any change. Anyway, this one time I was sitting on the line at Skipton in Yorkshire. We were kept waiting a short while for the previous race to clear. Once we were ready to go I put the bike in gear, throttle constant. The flag dropped, I let the clutch go and the bike shot backwards as I went straight over the handlebars, and all this without even leaving the line . . . makes you look really silly doesn't it!

'Then, there was the time at Bilstein in Germany where they had a pneumatic start gate that was impossible (well almost) to anticipate. Even over the noise of 50 screaming 125s you could hear the bang and feel the shudder as it went down. On top of the control tower there was a large clock. When the clock reached 12 o'clock I had worked out that the gate would drop about ten seconds later. I shall never forget this one occasion. We were all sitting on the line, bikes screaming away, concentrating like mad, ready to go. Just as the second hand was running up to the last few seconds before the clock reached midday, a tiny hand appeared from behind the clock face and held the second hand. I couldn't believe it. There was some little kid up there behind the clock, holding up the start of the German 125 cc GP. . . !'

4 First corner

This is simply a continuation of the principle of full commitment from the start. There are usually two lines to choose from, going into the corner. The first is up the inside, so if there is any bunching up or pushing, then it is you doing the leaning rather than getting T-boned. Also, if necessary, you can induce bunching up from that position by trying to, for instance, crowd a guy out who is alongside but outside you. Alternatively, you can take the wide line right around the outside. In some cases this can be the quicker line as well as offering the chance to steer clear of any possible trouble or first corner pile-ups on the inside line. The dive into the corner is the same technique for any corner, depending on whether it is a berm or flat-type corner. Now read on. . . .

5 Acceleration

Experienced racers say that you are always performing either of two operations when you are *racing*. Either *accelerating* to gain momentum as quickly as possible or trying to reverse the effect that acceleration causes by *braking* for all you're worth!

Air time on a motorcycle is usually lost time. Every position you get yourself into on the track should be planned to give you the maximum effective acceleration time. Have you noticed how ther fastest riders rarely 'look' like the fastest riders. Twice World 500 cc Champion Dave Thorpe is a classic example of a rider who never jumps the highest or furthest, or broadsides his bike out of corners in the most spectacular fashion or looks the fastest, but, boy does he get around the track mighty quick!

Make the maximum use of your acceleration time and you will gain speed around the track and improved lap times. The most effective way to achieve maximum acceleration is to adopt the seated attack position where possible and use full power gear changes, rather than lose time by opening and shutting the throttle. You can alter the amount of traction and spin by moving your backside up or down the saddle. Moving your weight back will give you more grip. Moving it forwards will give you more spin.

Keep your head over the pivot point (the steering head) where possible, elbows up and arms slightly bent. In that position any kicks or drifts can be corrected without the whole of your body being pulled all over the place and upsetting your balance. Your co-ordination is helped if you can keep your head as still as possible and over the pivot point. If you slide back down the saddle, taking your head behind the pivot point, any sudden slides or kicks will cause your body to be pulled about and eventually your head too. If your head is flung about, you will find co-ordination and control very difficult.

To find grip in muddy going you might have to move down the saddle, taking your head past the pivot point. If the bike does suddenly find a lot of grip and the bike slides, then as just described, your whole body will be moved making control very difficult and possibly causing you to high-side. Therefore the positioning of your behind on the saddle is a matter of compromise. Go back as far as you have to in order to find traction, but be aware of the problems this could cause in the event of finding sudden grip.

Where possible you should accelerate while in a seated attack position. If the ground is choppy though, as occurs where acceleration bumps have formed on the exit of certain corners, you will need to adjust quickly to a standing position in order to be able to keep your momentum going. The first bump you encounter can be used to knock you to your feet rather than expending energy unnecessarily by pulling yourself out of the saddle.

6 Berm corners

Successful berm cornering is all about commitment to the corner. You've got to throw the bike over on the floor and get it really low. The only thing that is then going to stop you falling flat on your face is to accelerate, which consequently makes you fast around the corner.

There are two main types of berm: firstly, the sort that is big enough and long enough to ride around; and secondly, the smaller, shorter, flatter berm that can be squared off.

Approach the berm standing in the attack position and brake deep into the corner with a precise idea of the exact point where you intend to hit the berm first. You can brake a long way into the berm because you want to keep the wheels as close to 90 degrees to the ground as possible. At the last possible moment before hitting the berm, change your riding position so that you are sitting down and upright in the middle of the bike, with your inside foot out and forward in line with the bike. You should keep your foot just off the ground, with your toes pointing forward, so that if it does touch down, it will slide. Holding your inside foot in this position helps your balance and keeps your foot out of the way while the bike is laid over. If it is a big, long berm, this position will also allow you to lean back slightly, so that you can glance at the exit of the corner and hold your head up to see if anyone has fallen off into your path.

A good rider should always have good track awareness, looking around and ahead for any riders that are down. Not only will you have the chance to change your line but this should also allow you to quickly assess just why they might have fallen off. Did they hit some hidden root or rock you can avoid next time around? If you are racing behind someone, leave yourself an alternative line where possible in case they go down. You will soon learn which riders are potential 'crashers' and which are a safer bet to follow into a line.

You can try a couple of methods for braking into the berm. To help prevent front wheel wash-out, keep one-finger pressure on the front brake with a little weight forward, right into the corner. This helps to draw the front tyre into the berm. The front tyre should collect the berm fractionally before the rear but don't lay the bike over until the rear picks up the berm too. At this point you will need speed to keep you upright. Effectively, riding around a berm is like riding on a straight because your wheels are still at 90 degrees to the ground. If you can master the technique of just how low your bike has to be for the speed you want, then you can improve your speed around the corner. As you go quicker you will have to get the bike lower to stay on it.

An alternative technique if you can master it, particularly for shorter berms, is to brake into the berm, locking the back wheel (making sure you whip in the clutch to prevent stalling), and drifting in so that both wheels hit the berm at the same time. At the precise moment of impact, let the clutch go as you accelerate to launch the bike out of the corner, together with a directional change.

As you approach the exit point of the corner on flatter ground, transfer some weight forward as you move back into the seated attack position. This will keep your weight forward and make the front tyre grip if you are still turning, and will keep the front end down for acceleration.

Get your head down over the front (similar to the position for starts) so that as much of your body as possible is over the pivot point, the steering head, rather than dragging behind it. Thus if the bike does start to fish-tail as you come out of the corner, then your body won't be pulled around so much and the bike will be easier to control. You must also be ready to move around quickly on the bike, transferring from the sitting-back position to an attack position. Be ready to move too if the corner is divided up into a berm, a little flat ground and another berm, with possibly a direction change as well.

Another tip is to use the clutch in the corner to maintain the necessary angle. If the clutch is pulled in while you are in the middle of the corner and cranked over, the bike will fall inwards. However, if instead you slip the clutch, the bike will stay upright and so accelerate much faster round the corner. You might also find this clutch technique useful in those corners where the best speed through the corner is obtained

ABOVE LEFT
Diving into the approach to a berm corner and in the transition from the standing braking position, with weight well back, to sitting down for the corner (*Adam Duckworth*)

LEFT
Sitting down on the outside of the bike with elbows up, inside leg coming forward, eyes fixed on intended point of impact in the berm, and bike beginning to be leaned over (*Adam Duckworth*)

ABOVE
Point of impact, with the bike heeled over and power being applied. Roger is leaning back slightly and looking for the exit from the corner. His weight is on the outer edge of the saddle and right side of the bike, his left leg being pointed forwards, but just off the ground. Both arms are bent and the outside elbow is up to keep the front tyre gripping the wall of the berm (*Adam Duckworth*)

ABOVE LEFT
Starting to exit the berm with the body in a
similar position, and beginning to accelerate
(*Adam Duckworth*)

LEFT
Accelerating hard and moving weight forwards
towards the pivot point in order to be ready for
any slide. Note how Roger keeps his left boot
tucked behind the footrest at this critical stage of
acceleration, to keep it from getting snagged in the
rear wheel (*Adam Duckworth*)

ABOVE
Full power as the bike becomes upright and body
leaning slightly, in this instance, to correct a small
slide. Left boot is back on the footrest, ready to
change gear, while elbows and head are up just
prior to getting into the attack position (*Adam
Duckworth*)

by using a higher gear—with the clutch.

Berm technique can also be used in a variety of other, slightly alternative ways. One of Britain's current top 500 cc GP riders, Kurt Nicoll, had some learning to do in his earlier days when he came up against Roger Harvey who generously demonstrated one form of the technique to Kurt. Roger can pick up the story.

'During Kurt Nicoll's 125 cc days we were vying for a place during a particular race at Streatley Hills. Kurt was behind me. He was faster than me but I was cannier. As the race went on Kurt was slowly catching me up. With just a couple of laps to go he had caught me up and was trying to get past. He followed me on the same line into a corner that had a well-formed, deep berm. Halfway around the berm I whipped my clutch in and just touched the back brake, slowing for a fraction of a second before accelerating again. It was enough for Kurt's front tyre to touch my rear, sending him crashing to the ground.

'Needless to say this secured the position for me and afterwards I went up to Kurt to discuss how unfortunate it had all been, what with the way my bike had missed a gear like that *and* all in the middle of the corner. . . How unlucky. Kurt, who was riding for Kawasaki, was quite naive and inexperienced in those days, and was agreeing with me about the untimeliness of it all when Alec Wright, who had seen what had happened, overheard us and rushed up.

"Bullshit, ace. . ." he growled at me, and dragged a very young and green, Kurt away, telling him he wasn't ever to pay attention to a single word I said. . .'

Kurt also features in another story, this time at Farleigh Castle. Again, Roger was trying to find ways of slowing him down. This time he chose to play on the motocross rider's apparently frail confidence and picked on a habit of Kurt's that he had noticed of riding sitting right up on the tank, even on steep downhills.

After the first race, when Kurt had beaten him, Roger sauntered up to Kurt for a 'chat'. During the meandering conversation he gave Kurt the benefit of his considerable experience and warned him how (for his own sake and well-being of course) he was heading for a big fall if he carried on sitting right up, especially on the big, steep downhills. All the time he was trying to pysche Kurt out enough to plant the seed of nagging doubt in his mind so that he would go slower in the race.

Kurt's father, Dave, himself a former top motocrosser during the 'Swinging Sixties', was working on Kurt's bike and overheard Roger trying to wind him up. (Why did everyone always eavesdrop on Roger chatting, on the surface quite innocently, to their young up-and-coming protégés?) He too rushed up and pulled Kurt away, directing various profanities in Roger's general direction, and telling Kurt he wasn't to pay any attention to any of it.

In the following sequence, Roger is approaching a more established berm in a seated position, having just accelerated up a small rise leading to the corner. Notice that neither brake is being operated in this case, as the berm will take account of his approach speed (*Vic Barnes*)

ABOVE
This could almost be a case of spot the point of impact, as the rider's head is fixed on the point at which he intends to hit the berm (*Vic Barnes*)

ABOVE RIGHT
Note the excellent body position in terms of all the rider's weight being on the right-hand side of the machine, elbow up, and angle of the bike in relation to the ground (*Vic Barnes*)

RIGHT
See how high the front tyre is on the face of the berm just prior to the point of impact and how the inside leg is held out merely to help balance and as a stabilizer (*Vic Barnes*)

7 Flat corners

Flat corners are one of the places on the track where good style and technique can shine out and are a favourite for action photographs. Fast, fluid motion and a good rooster tail capture for me one of the less brutal and more beautiful aspects of off-road riding technique.

Flat corners require a very similar technique to berm corners. They should be approached in the attack position standing up on the pegs with your bum over the back of the bike and with two fingers only on the front brake. All the weight is thrown on to the front of the bike, so by keeping your weight over the back you should stop yourself getting thrown over the front.

Use your front brake to the limit and keep the rear merely for control and manoeuvring the bike. Get all your heavy braking done before you pitch the bike over, otherwise it is liable to slide away from you. In some instances you can set the bike drifting into the corner which helps to scrub more speed off.

Go into the corner as deeply as possible, leaning the bike into the corner while keeping your body more upright (unlike body positioning in a berm corner where you lean with the bike). Then sit down in the middle of the bike with your weight on the outside edge of the saddle, right up against the seat/tank join and your inside leg pointing forward in the direction you are going. Pressing weight on your outside leg, planted firmly on the footrest, will help you find grip.

Keep your outside elbow up and your inside elbow slightly bent with your head over the front to keep the front wheel pushed into the ground. Apply smooth throttle, depending on track conditions and camber, allowing the back end to drift a little if necessary.

Remember to keep your head over the pivot point as you accelerate out of the corner to prevent your body being pulled around and control any slides or drifts with a combination of the throttle and clutch. Arching your back while keeping your elbows up on acceleration will help to keep your bum on the bike, but be ready to shift your weight forwards or backwards on the saddle to find the maximum traction and therefore speed.

The quickest rider around a flat corner is the one who times his braking just right and rides the corner fluently, rather than the do-or-die merchants who feel that the harder they try, the faster they will go. Again, think back to your own experience. Who wins the races?—the genuinely fast riders who keep up the same pace throughout a race, or the apparently fast rider who strings a couple of laps or corners together well but hasn't got the technique to keep it going for the whole race?

ABOVE LEFT
You can clearly see the dust kicked up as Roger hit the berm and accelerated to get his speed around the corner (*Vic Barnes*)

LEFT
Starting to accelerate out of the corner, while keeping the outside elbow up to keep weight on the front tyre, aid steering and to stop it washing out as power is applied (*Vic Barnes*)

TOP
Warren is demonstrating the classic braking position up to this flat corner, with two fingers on the front brake and using the rear merely for control. He is keeping his weight well back, his elbows bent and his wrists in line with his arms (*Adam Duckworth*)

ABOVE
Beginning to ease off the brakes, particularly the front, as he starts to lean the bike over into the corner and sit down near the front of the saddle (*Adam Duckworth*)

TOP
The front of the bike is still loaded as it is leaned into the corner. The inside boot is being pointed forwards (it would normally by more pointed than this but Warren was wearing brand-new boots that had yet to be broken in!) and the power is just beginning to be fed in (*Adam Duckworth*)

ABOVE
Warren is starting to power out of the corner— notice the front suspension unloading - and is in the correct position to control any slide that may develop as he accelerates (*Adam Duckworth*)

ABOVE

This switch to Roger from the outside of the corner demonstrates more clearly the body positioning needed to control the bike in a flat corner. Here, we can see the body positioned on the outside of the bike and the left footrest weighted, while the outside elbow is up to keep the front tyre pushed into the ground and maintain grip as the bike is leaned over

ABOVE RIGHT AND RIGHT

If you drift the bike out of the corner, you need to be in the right position. These two pictures show Roger accelerating hard out of the corner with his elbows up and his head forward towards the pivot point. Although the bike is drifting, Roger's head has not and remains over the steering head

8   Ramp jumps

For the sake of technique, we will define a ramp jump as a normal, straightforward jump preceded by an uphill ramp with the landing taking place on flat ground.

Initially, the best way to tackle a ramp jump is to imagine you are riding along a flat, straight section of track. Keep the bike flexible underneath you. Don't grip it too tightly with your legs, don't adjust the throttle and don't pull on the bars as you take-off. That way you can be assured of a good angle on take-off and your rear wheel should come down just ahead of your front wheel, and still be rotating as you land.

The next stage is to build in taking-off and listening for the engine revs to pick up as you get airborne, shutting-off while in mid-air and bringing the power back in just before you land to ensure an easier landing and a quick getaway. These jumps are normally best tackled in a standing position with the rider neutrally placed in the middle of the bike, ready to apply any body adjustments should they be required on take-off or in mid-air.

If the ramp is quite small, a useful technique is to loft the front wheel on to the ramp in order to take the sting out of the back of the bike and to keep the bike lower through the air, thus making it faster. This is not an easy technique; if you lift the front wheel too early and miss the top of the ramp you run the risk of cartwheeling down the track. This could hurt and is not generally recommended.

The only time you should sit down for a jump is because of lack of time and *not* fatigue! This could occur, for example, where coming out of a corner, you simply haven't enough time to get out of the saddle before having to tackle a jump. Remember, a standing position will always give you more control. Problems can occur on this type of jump in three main ways:

1   The rider blips the throttle at the end of the ramp and lofts the front wheel. This usually means landing with the front wheel too high. This not only loses time but makes the bike harder to control.

2   The rider shuts off too soon, effectively applying a brake—if only engine braking. This will pull the front wheel downwards, causing the bike to nose dive. If this happens, gripping the bike with your legs might help you to stay on. Also, if there is time, opening the throttle while in mid-air will pull the back of the bike down.

Either (**1**) or (**2**) can lead to your third problem: landing with the throttle shut.

3   If you land from any type of jump with the throttle shut you will be landing with a brake on the engine. As a result, when the bike lands everything is thrown forward, including the humble rider! This usually results in either a spectacular high-sider causing the rider to disappear over the bars, or a huge wobble, both of which are very entertaining for those watching, but not a great deal of fun for the vexed rider!

TOP RIGHT
The ramp jump is probably the 'classic' jump—jumping off a ramp, preceded by and followed by a flat straight. In this sequence, Warren demonstrates the approach position with his body relaxed, arms slightly bent and elbows up, knees bent and head in line with the steering head. This position will remain largely unchanged for the whole jump (*Adam Duckworth*)

CENTRE RIGHT
The suspension is compressed as the rider prepares to take-off and his body is slightly more upright (*Adam Duckworth*)

RIGHT
The rider's weight is moved back as he takes some of the kick from the take-off ramp with his legs. The angle of the bike is still the same as the take-off ramp (*Adam Duckworth*)

ABOVE
The bike flattens out at the mid point of the jump and the rider's weight is still towards the back of the bike (*Adam Duckworth*)

ABOVE RIGHT
As the bike begins to come down, the rider's weight is brought forward a little and his legs straightened in order to assure a rear-wheel landing (*Adam Duckworth*)

RIGHT
Just as the rear tyre makes contact, the power is brought in to load the rear suspension and maintain momentum, while the rider's legs are bent to help make a smooth landing. Note the body position and the head still in line with the steering head, just as it was for the approach (*Adam Duckworth*)

9 Table-top jumps

Table-top jumps come in various shapes and sizes. Correct air-shape over them is what you are trying to achieve. Suspension compression will help you do this.

You can compress, or pre-load, your suspension from either a standing, or seated, position. Hitting the approach ramp seated will compress the suspension more than if you are standing, but you can also load the suspension by using your legs like springs on the ramp to squash the suspension. Once you start to clear the take-off ramp your suspension will extend, launching you into the air.

Until you are confident you have perfected the technique, for the sake of safety, keep a higher gear than you might normally want to on the approach. This is not for speed, but because your engine will be slightly less responsive than it would be in a lower gear. Thus the last blip of the throttle on take-off can't have such a marked effect that it flips the bike backwards making landing very heavy and very, very difficult!

Only experience and practice will teach you what gear, revs, and speed are needed to clear a particular obstacle but you should aim at landing front wheel down on the landing ramp, thus achieving a good curved air-shape with a comfortable, light landing easy on rider and bike alike. Get the power on just before the rear wheel touches the ground, partly for speed but also because landing on a closed throttle is like landing with a brake on, which might tip you over the bars as the suspension is allowed to compress. The acceleration on landing will prevent the rear suspension, in particular, from compressing fully and losing you valuable acceleration time.

Bear in mind that if you do flip the bike backwards on take-off, pulling the clutch in, and applying the rear brake while in mid-air, will have the effect of bringing the front down again. Conversely, if the front is too low, opening the throttle while in mid-air will have the effect of bringing the back of the bike down. With loads and loads of practice, these tips will become second nature to you.

They obviously only apply, however, if you are still in contact with your bike and in a position to save it (see the section on crashing for further advice!).

ABOVE
His legs are straightened to further load the suspension while his body is still positioned centrally on the bike (*Adam Duckworth*)

ABOVE
The bike is still on its way skywards in this shot, and Warren is making a minor body adjustment to maintain a straight trajectory. The approach speed will determine the distance and the loading of the suspension on the take-off ramp, plus the height of the jump in order to make the necessary distance (*Adam Duckworth*)

TOP
This is the mid point of the jump and, in this instance, Warren has whipped his clutch in and is applying the rear brake to bring the front of the bike down for a good approach to landing. You can see that the rear wheel spokes have stopped rotating while the front wheel is still turning. He has also moved his weight towards the back, to prepare for the landing (*Adam Duckworth*)

ABOVE
You can see that the front wheel is dropping while the rear brake is on. The time gap in this sequence is only a matter of a second or so, and the rear brake is released as soon as it has the desired effect (*Adam Duckworth*)

ABOVE
This particular table top has a span of about four bike lengths. Looks easy, doesn't it? (*Adam Duckworth*)

ABOVE RIGHT
The rider's weight is to the rear as he comes in to land so that he doesn't get thrown forward. He is looking to get both wheels down at about the same time (*Adam Duckworth*)

RIGHT
Touchdown! The rider's weight is in the middle of the bike and both front and rear suspension are compressed as the power is brought back in on landing. The knees and ankles have been used to help control on landing and avoid any jarring (*Adam Duckworth*)

10 Jumping

Jumping uphill

In certain instances you will be better off jumping up the whole, or part, of a hill rather than simply riding up it. For example, you may want to clear natural obstacles, such as the steps in the big hill at Farleigh Castle, or you may want an alternative line, like the inside line up the hill after the start at the National Motocross and Trials Park Supercross track at Worcester. The technique can also be used to save time going up rough, lumpy hills.

Approach the obstacle in the standing attack position with your weight in the middle of the bike, focusing on the take-off point and aiming to use a lot of pre-jump off the ramp or a bump, hopefully to lift the bike right to the top of the hill or your chosen

objective. Keep your knees bent as the suspension compresses and treat the take-off as you would a normal jump. This means keeping a constant throttle and aiming to land the front wheel just higher than the back—so avoiding disappearing over the bars when you do land.

Just before take-off, straighten your legs to load the suspension even further to give you maximum lift. Let the back-end kick quite hard off the ramp and float the bike up the hill. Your wheels will be roughly parallel to the slope so even if you do land short of the top, you will still be safe. You should try to land at the top of the hill with your wheels virtually flat to the ground, ready to make your turn.

BELOW LEFT
Rob is approaching this uphill jump in a good attacking position with his elbows up, knees bent and head in line with the steering head. He has already assessed the speed he will need to clear the hill and is accelerating hard up to the ramp (*Adam Duckworth*)

BELOW
The suspension compresses as the bike starts to hit the ramp, while Rob maintains a similar body position (*Adam Duckworth*)

ABOVE
Just as the front is about to clear the ramp, Rob straightens his legs and further squashes the rear suspension to maximize the amount of lift he will get (*Adam Duckworth*)

ABOVE RIGHT
With the rear still as compressed as Rob can get it, the front starts to get airborne (*Adam Duckworth*)

RIGHT
Time to take to the air! Rob has shifted his weight towards the back of the bike and is at the mid point of his jump uphill. The bike is still roughly parallel to the hill and you can see that he has (finally) shut the throttle (*Adam Duckworth*)

ABOVE
Rob is looking for his landing point as the bike starts to flatten in the air (*Adam Duckworth*)

ABOVE RIGHT
Preparing for touchdown. Rob has kept his weight back, as the front is going to land just ahead of the rear and the throttle is still shut (makes a change) (*Adam Duckworth*)

RIGHT
Rob brings the power back on (again) a fraction of a second before he lands and prepares to demolish a sharp left-hand berm at the top of the hill (*Adam Duckworth*)

Jumping downhill

The first rule for jumping downhill successfully is to be always sure that you have enough room to land while there is still some hill left! It sounds obvious, but if you do jump down off a hill and land flat in the bottom you run the risk of wrecking yourself and the bike. Bear in mind that you are aiming to keep the wheels parallel to the hill in mid-air, while still allowing yourself time to land on the last downhill section.

Accelerate up to the corner preceding the hill (assuming there is one) in the attack position. Allow for slight braking into the corner at the top of the hill and then accelerate off the top, shutting off at the last minute in order to bring the front end down and to give you the right air-shape for your descent. Let the bike float downhill until the back wheel and then front wheel are on the floor and you are fully in control of the bike and able to accelerate up to the next obstacle. If you do need to use braking at the bottom, use both your rear and front brakes, but use the front very cautiously.

Start on smaller hills until you are confident and sufficiently skilled enough to attack the really big and gnarly hills. Don't be intimidated by the size of a hazard. If you are safe and your technique is good, it won't matter how big or bad it is—you can be badder!

Angled take—off/landing

If a jump is on a corner, the take-off is in one direction and the landing is in another completely different direction. Obviously you are unable to turn the bike much in the air, so the take-off will determine your direction in flight. You can use body input and move the bike over in the air to a certain extent, or keep it in the air for a fraction longer, such as you would for say, a rider off in front of you, or some other hazard you would want to avoid, but take-off is crucial in normal circumstances.

Approach the take-off ramp as for a normal jump, but at the very last minute, start to make your manoeuvre. For instance, if the corner turns to the left, approach in a straight line to the right-hand side of the approach to the corner and turn very slightly left on the last piece of the ramp. The bike will tend to follow that curve when you actually take off. You can also pull the bike round a little while airborne to help you make the turn. This is where the spectacular 'cross-ups' originated from—riders trying to force their bikes round physically while in mid-air. It looks really neat and stylish, but is actually slower than keeping a low and flat trajectory through the air and getting back to terra firma as quickly as possible.

ABOVE RIGHT
Warren is accelerating towards this particular downhill jump, but is making sure that he is not going too fast for the hill. He needs enough speed to jump downhill, but still leave himself some of the slope to land on

RIGHT
He moves into a standing position and still has the power on as he begins to take off

TOP
A perfect take-off has meant that there is no need for any body adjustment and Warren can maintain a 'neutral' body position in the middle of the bike, with the throttle closed. Note how both wheels are almost parallel to the hill

ABOVE
The bike is coming in to land with the rear wheel fractionally ahead of the front as Warren adjusts his body position towards the back of the bike

TOP
Just before the rear wheel makes contact, the power is applied to ensure that no speed is lost and that the bike doesn't land with engine braking, which might throw the rider forwards. Note the rider's weight is towards the back of the bike as he lands, but his head is still in line with the steering head.

ABOVE
This is a good shot to illustrate the body position for landing, and you can see that Warren is gassing the bike to reduce the rear suspension sag and to keep his speed up to the next corner

11   Braking and acceleration bum

Braking bumps are always good value from a spectator's point of view because it is amazing how many good riders come to grief on them. Technically they are not difficult if you concentrate. Perhaps the riders who fall off are concentrating on the corner so hard that they forget to think about the relatively easy bumps on the approach.

Braking bumps should be approached in the normal braking position but try to enter the hazard in a higher gear and then drop into the gear you want for the corner, as you actually arrive in the corner. That way you will have on less engine brake, allowing your rear suspension to work and avoiding some of the bad kicks from the back of the bike. Keep your weight right back while braking, again in order to take some of the kick out of the bike and also to avoid going over the front (what, again. . . !) if you are braking really heavily. Be careful with the use of the front brake to make sure you don't drop the front wheel into a hole where it would be likely to lock up. Get the braking bumps out of the way and only then dive into the corner.

Acceleration bumps require similar body positioning. You should be in the attack position, with your weight right over the rear, avoiding rear-wheel drift where possible. Come out of the corner preceding the bumps with the front and rear wheels following the same path, otherwise the rear tyre could hook up on the face of the first bump and pitch you off. Moving from a seated position in the corner to a standing attack position for the bumps can be made easier by hitting the first bump and using it to knock you out of the saddle and on to your feet. This is also an energy-saving technique that can be used in a number of instances to 'help you to your feet'.

Accelerating over choppy ground, or sometimes simply trying to, can also be made easier by exactly the same technique and body positioning used for acceleration bumps out of a corner, and it is a lot quicker than the alternative pin-it-and-hang-on technique so often seen which is not only unreliable, but tiring too.

12   Whoops

Whoops are a common obstacle and are found in just about every modern track in some form or other. They can be tackled in two ways. The first method is to tackle two or three at a time, treating them as small table tops or doubles. (There used to be a lot of double jumps in their own right but these are now banned. The technique, however, is exactly the same as that for table-top jumps which are like a double jump that has been filled in.) Make the first whoop your take-off ramp, jump and land downhill in between two bumps before using the next uphill to take-off again. Feet should be properly on the footrests with the rider in the middle of the bike on take-off, ready to get his weight over the back on landing.

For smaller whoops, a sometimes faster technique is accelerating down them. Jump into the whoops on

ABOVE RIGHT
This series of whoops can be tackled in a variety of ways. In this sequence, Roger jumps into the gap between the first two whoops so that he can use the face of the second whoop to attack the series ahead of him (*Vic Barnes*)

RIGHT
This shows the positioning as the rider accelerates off the top of one whoop and squashes the rear suspension—elbows up, head over the steering head and front wheel lofted towards the next whoop (*Vic Barnes*)

TOP
Notice how the front wheel stays almost in line with the rope in the background as the bike is aimed at the next whoop (*Vic Barnes*)

ABOVE
Again, you can see that the front wheel has stayed at roughly the same height and that the rear suspension is now fully extended just before it hits the face of the next whoop (*Vic Barnes*)

TOP
If the front wheel doesn't make it all the way to the next whoop, you will need to be ready to put your weight right over the back of the bike, making sure you keep your arms slightly bent and the front straight. Many riders come off in this type of situation, when they lose control and the front wheel tucks in under the front of the bike, tipping the rider over the handlebars (*Vic Barnes*)

ABOVE
Still in charge, Roger prepares to hammer through the remaining three whoops (*Vic Barnes*)

the first one, then accelerate hard down the entire length, keeping your weight well back and arms slightly bent. Try to keep the front wheel just off the ground the whole time, barely skimming the tops of the bumps and making your rear suspension work really hard coping with the hits from the faces of the bumps. If you do adopt this method, don't whatever you do decide halfway down them that you want to shut off, because your front wheel will disappear in one of the holes, turfing you off.

To learn this method, try building up to it by using the last two whoops in a series, and then the last three and so on, until you feel confident enough to attack the whole lot.

Keeping the balls of your feet on the footrests will allow you to get your feet and thus weight even further back, and will also utilise whatever suspension your legs and ankles have to offer. The balls of your feet, not toes, must be properly planted on the footrests, otherwise you might slip off which can lead to a very painful and a very, very unstylish dumping off the bike!

Never renowned for his stadium technique, but admired for his determination and technique on traditional motocross tracks was the world famous 'Carla'—Hakan Carlqvist. During his career, Roger met and raced against him in numerous different situations. One occasion that stands out was the time Roger bumped into him down under in Australia.

'During the winter of 1983–4, I was doing a series of Stadium Cross in Australia and one of the other Europeans out there was Carla. There was a line of nine whoops that you had to do as two, two, two and three, but you had to work really hard to get the last three. The Aussies were getting through them OK and Paul Hunt and I, the only Brits over there, were also doing them without too much trouble, but Carla was having distinct problems. All he kept saying was: "bloody 250s, no power, so small. I don't know how you can ride these things. . ." Anyway, we all had a good time watching Carla practising and trying to do the whoops properly. He was getting all the timing wrong and was being wound up too by the other riders who were telling him how well he was doing the whoops and all that, when he knew full well that he wasn't getting them right at all.

'On the final practice he decided he had enough of trying the stadium method, he would now try the Carla method. He came around the corner, lifted the front wheel and hammered down the entire length of the whoops on the back wheel while keeping the front wheel skimming the tops. If you look at Ricky Johnson today, he uses a similar technique for the big whoops. But Carla was magic and came in from practice with a huge grin spread all over his face as if to say to the rest of us—well, what about that then!'

TOP
This is another shot of the same place from a different angle, showing the correct body position on the approach run (*Vic Barnes*)

ABOVE
Roger is now standing and is loading the rear suspension to help give him lift when he takes off. Elbows are still up and arms bent to help maintain control (*Vic Barnes*)

TOP
The front wheel is clear and Roger's weight has moved towards the rear and his legs are straight to keep the rear suspension loaded (*Vic Barnes*)

ABOVE
Take-off! Now all thoughts are on achieving a good landing on the downside of the far hump (*Vic Barnes*)

ABOVE
The air shape is looking good as Roger shifts his weight right to the back of the bike (while still keeping his arms slightly bent) and pushes the front wheel towards its intended target (*Vic Barnes*)

ABOVE RIGHT
Objective successfully achieved. The front has cleared the hump and the rear is following right behind, although his weight is still kept to the back of the bike (*Vic Barnes*)

RIGHT
The dust trail indicates where Roger has put the power back on just as the rear wheel landed, and he has already accelerated towards the next obstacle (*Vic Barnes*)

13   Passing

This is a short section because you do it as quickly as you can rather than stopping behind someone. If you hang around the guy in front, invariably you find yourself concentrating on their back mudguard and your speed drops to their pace. As you come up to someone, zap them as they appear, don't wait, don't deliberate over it, do it!

There are obviously safer places to overtake than others. For instance, don't try to take someone around the outside when you can dive up the inside, and take him on the ground where you can make up time rather than in the air where you can lose it.

What would you do if you had a future double world champion sitting on your tail shouting at you to move out of his way? If you were Roger Harvey, you would calmly ignore him! Read on. . .

'During the early '80s, a youngster, David Thorpe, was starting to go quite quickly. When we met this time, during a round of the 500 cc British Championship at Lyng, he and I were going about the same pace, but I was in front of him. Dave was trying every way to get past me. If he came up the inside, I would tend to go straight on, to force him out. Anyway, Dave was getting a little upset by all of this and was shouting and screaming ". . . get out of my way . . ." as well as a selection of other suggestions as to what I might do.

'Meanwhile I was just riding along in front of him, using the track as a "crafty" technician would use the track, using track craft (blocking) and basically using all the track! Eventually he did manage to get past me

and started to pull away for a couple of laps.

Unfortunately for Dave a stone came up and knocked his petrol pipe off, causing him to run out of fuel and allowing me to keep my placing after all. He came up to me afterwards moaning at me for blocking him.

"David" I said "we were both in the same race, both on the same lap. I was in front of you on that lap, so, when you are racing me, don't bother shouting at me because I won't move. If you are lapping me, shout and I will move." There was some further discussion over the matter, but the point was duly taken.

'Later that same year, during the 125 cc British Championship at Beenham Park, Thorpe was brought in by Kawasaki as part of a block tactic. Jonathan Wright and I were fighting it out for the title. Dave was on a real trick bike and his instructions before the race were to block me.

'I got a bad start and was fourth on the opening lap. Quite quickly I got up to third behind Dave, with Jonathan leading. To win the championship, I had to beat Jonathan. Pit boards were going out to Thorpe, "Block Harvey", "Slow Harvey" etc. I was up behind Thorpe, trying everything to get past him. Up the inside, around the outside, banging him, shouting at him to get out of the way, everything I could. Anyway, I couldn't get past him and eventually finished third. I was really sick, especially at the way it had been done. Afterwards Dave came up to see me and I had a moan at him for getting in my way and blocking me. "Roger" he said pausing for a moment "if you're lapping me . . ." The point had indeed been taken!'

14   Braking

Braking, after acceleration, is the main aspect of your riding that can sort out the good riders from the average and give you speed around the track. Correct technique is essential for controlled and effective braking. The do-or-die, leave it to the last second, jam on the anchors and stuff it sideways into the corner (or a hapless opponent. . .) approach might work occasionally. But it is like placing your luck in an hourglass—okay for a limited period of time, but bound to run out sooner or later!

You should always brake standing in the classic attack position, except for your weight being back and your head behind the steering head, with your arms up, knees and elbows bent, and concentrating on your braking point up to and into the corner. A useful energy-saving technique is to keep your wrists in a line with your forearms; this will help to prevent wrist fatigue.

The heavy braking should be done upright and with your body in a straight line. Most of the weight is on the front so most of the braking should be carried out using the front brake, keeping the rear for control of the back of the bike and balance. Use two fingers only for the front brake so that you will still be able to grip the handlebars with your two other fingers (and hopefully your thumb!).

Stay relaxed and loose by not gripping the bike too tightly with your legs—feel through the footrests what the bike is doing. Never take your whole foot off the rest to operate the rear brake: it's a sure way to stall the bike. Use the inner edge of your boot (where the base of your big toe should be lurking. . .) on the brake pedal only. Your instep should remain on the footrest to act as a pivot point.

Don't sit down to brake. If you do, you are likely to slide right up the tank, forcing you to take your foot off the rest to use the back brake. This in turn will make you more likely to lock up the back wheel and possibly stall the bike, as well as giving you less control over the whole of the bike than if you were in the correct standing position.

Be ready to use the clutch if necessary on the final approach to the corner, or if you need to lock up the back wheel to bring the back end round in the corner. Normally the clutch would be left out all the way into the turn, ready to be slipped if required to keep up momentum once the bike is in the corner.

'It's marvellous what experience can do.'—This was Roger's conclusion to a story he told me about braking, or rather the devious art of brake testing as practised on a certain young, up-and-coming Mayson Wear, one fine day at Hawkstone Park, Roger's 'home' track. . .

'It was New Year's Day at Hawkstone Park in the days when the big double was still in—a thing I would have loved to do, but never had the bottle. I was never brave enough to do it, but then I'm still here today. . . Anyway, on this particular occasion, I landed in the sand-pit alongside Mayson Wear and I saw him look across at me and think "I'm going to race you!" So we accelerated together up towards the double jump and both left the throttle on as long as possible, waiting for the other to shut off. At the last moment I whipped the clutch in but kept the throttle pinned for a split second, which meant that Mayson went flat out another yard further than I did.

'I went over the first part of the double, landed down the down ramp and took off again before landing on the other side. Mayson, meanwhile, because he'd gone that extra yard, had taken off and slammed straight into the other side. His head shot forward and banged the handlebars until his suspension recoiled and then he bounced skywards again off the second jump. He was launched right up into the air before landing completely off the track, up by the chestnut paling where the fence was quite high. He then bounced back down on to the track and landed right alongside me. I was howling with laughter because he'd fallen for it hook, line and sinker. I turned round to look at him.

'His face mask had been knocked up and had hit the top of his helmet so that he was looking out of two little slits, and there was blood pouring out from underneath, where he had banged his chin on the handlebars. Fair dues to him though, he came up to me later and fought back by saying, "I suppose, Roger, that's what's known as experience. . ."'

15   Crashing

If you are going to play on motorbikes off-road, you know that at some time or other you are going to crash. When that point of no return is reached, you want to make sure, where possible, that you get away from your bike and that *it* doesn't get entangled with *you*. Most of the time you can crash quite 'successfully', and not hurt yourself until the bike hits you.

If you are going over the bars, try and push off to one side, effectively pushing yourself one way and the bike another. Get your legs out of the way if you are going down on your side. Legs can get folded back, twisting feet right round and back, probably giving rise to knee problems. If, while you are racing, you hit something that throws you towards a post or tree, get your leg out of the way. I've seen people snap posts, but lift their leg out of harm's way, even ending up almost on just one side of the bike and still being able to carry on.

Do all you can to miss the post that seems to leap out in front of you. You have to be flexible on the bike. Try to stay with the bike if at all possible rather than abandoning ship at the first sign of trouble. We've all, I'm sure, been surprised at sometime just how we 'managed to save that one', but if the time comes when you *do* have to get off the bike, get off and away from it. Normally, if you have had to reach that hurried conclusion, it is big crash time and you want to be as far away from the bike as possible. The great Jeff Smith is said to have actually practised coming off his bike—not something to be recommended nowadays!

16   Play riding

This is something everyone should do. There is no need to do anything stupid or insanely radical, but just go and practise over jumps, cross the bike up, do pre-jumping down hills, just play and have fun on your motorbike. The reason you got the bike in the first place was to go out and have fun, so do precisely that!

Play riding teaches you things about your bike and your ability on that bike. It also teaches you how to cope with situations you might not normally get into while racing. It gives you the chance to experiment and see what your bike is really capable of in a relatively controlled and unstressed situation, away from the racing environment. So, if you get crossed-up, or in some other radical position during a race, then your brain can say—Wait a minute, I've been here before. I know about this. I *can* save it.

Practise trying to get your bike up on the front wheel using the front brake, it's good for control. Wheelies or near-vertical wheelies have a safety, as well as a skill, aspect to them. If you do get into that sort of position during a race then you are already conditioned to react to it.

Do your serious training for an hour-long session, then come in, fuel up, check the bike for loose spokes, nuts and bolts, tighten the chain and go out for another 45–60 minutes session. Come in again and then just go out and play for a while, even for another hour or so. Play riding is just as important to your riding technique and style as any amount of serious training around the track.

PART TWO

ENDURO RIDING TECHNIQUE

1 Enduro events

Enduros used to be called Timed Trials until quite recently, a title that described the nature of the sport a degree more aptly than its modern counterpart, which has a faintly butch and macho ring to it. The ACU handbook defines enduros as long-distance timed trials of endurance and reliability that don't include observed sections (such as you would find in trials events).

One of the beauties of enduros is that you can take the sport as seriously and competitively as *you* want to. There is no chequered flag for the winner to pass but a course marked out for you to follow. This is normally made up of unprepared tracks and cross-country going, broken down into sections with a check at each end, which you must ride in a certain time. You can incur the same penalty points for checking in too early as you can for riding into a check after your allotted time. The time for each section is worked out by the event organizers so that the speed between the checks doesn't exceed an average of 30 mph.

There are various classes available to you: Championship, for those competing in the British Enduro Championship; Expert, for those who think they could be competitive in the Championship class; and Clubman. This last class is the one that most riders enter under, and is meant for the average rider who has some experience of riding off-road but with neither the skill nor desire to compete at the same level as the top riders.

More and more riders are taking up the sport of enduro. Many come from other spheres of off-road motorcycle sport such as trials and motocross while many others are newcomers to off-road competition. They all find enduros offer good value, in terms of the available time to ride (normally a minimum of 4–5 hours), the relaxed camaraderie and atmosphere that come from it being a largely amateur sport, and the good overall motorcycling. As the name implies, there is an element of endurance to enduros and this varies according to the event and class you have entered. The better riders, Championship and Expert, have to ride further and harder than Clubman riders.

Quite recently a new class, Sportsman/Trail, has been introduced for riders with little or no off-road experience, and for owners of the increasingly popular, dual-purpose Trail bikes. These bikes are designed primarily for road use but can be ridden off road too, albeit with a good deal of restraint. Their suspension systems and chassis aren't made to take the same pounding that motocross or enduro bikes get, and must be ridden more slowly and gently. The schedule and course set by the organizers will reflect these limitations so don't worry about not being able to take part, whatever bike you ride!

There is obviously a lot more to entering enduros than I have mentioned here, but this book is intended to show you the techniques needed to ride enduros rather than how to get organized for them. The ACU is a good starting point and their handbook will also list your nearest affiliated motorcycle club. You should find them only too keen to welcome new members and give you all the help and advice you need to find out the rules and form of enduros. You can also find most events advertised in the weekly paper, *Trials and Motocross News*.

Although I hate sweeping statements, as a general rule, most enduro riders merely make do when it comes to their riding technique. They would do well to apply a little effort to make control of their steed a more managed affair. You don't need to try to ride like David Thorpe every time you go out on a section, but all enduro riders can use motocross technique to make their riding easier and more effective. The best place to learn the finer points of riding, particularly slower, tricky going, is undoubtedly trials riding. I am not saying that every one wanting to ride enduros will have to try these other sports to ride more effectively, but merely that good riding techniques and useful skills can be learnt from both disciplines.

The terrain you encounter riding enduros can vary enormously, and it would be impossible to pick out all the subtly differing techniques you would need for every type of obstacle you might come across. However, the techniques described in this part of the book will show you the right way to go about tackling most of the hazards you are likely to find on an enduro. It is essential that you read the motocross part first, however, as many of the body positions and techniques you will use in enduro riding have their roots in motocross.

My final note, before you get stuck into the enduro section, is to remember that no one is born with the skills necessary to go out and win Enduros; they have to be acquired and practised, and then practised some more. The very top riders put an immense amount of effort and dedication into their chosen sport and should be admired for it. At grass roots level the aim should be above all to enjoy your riding, and the enduro section aims to make that task a little easier for you.

2 Riding across branches

You are most likely to find this type of hazard in the middle of forests where a track has been cleared between the trees. This can cause you two immediate problems. Firstly, visibility can be limited by the shade of the trees, as well as by low hanging branches, particularly for taller riders. Secondly, if the course does cut a swathe through a copse of trees, then your avenues of escape are limited if you are diverted from your chosen path.

Where branches are laid flat across the track, the quicker you go across them, the better off you are likely to be. Try to assess the extent of the hazard ahead of you and approach it with caution. Stay loose on the bike and use either the standing or seated, motocross-type, attack position. Really try hard to keep relaxed, because apart from helping to save energy, this will allow your body to react more quickly and effectively than when all tensed up.

Riding over branches is just the kind of situation in which the bike is liable to dart away from you without warning as it skids off a branch or semi-hidden stump. If your elbows are down, then your whole body will

RIGHT
This is one of the trickiest hazards you can come across on an enduro, especially if it is wet, as it was for our photo session! It is essential to stay loose and relaxed on the bike and try to tackle the obstacle standing up on the footrests, as you will be able to exercise greater control (*Adam Duckworth*)

FAR RIGHT
Read ahead, where possible, to pick a route which avoids branches that are at too much of an angle, as these will whip your front wheel away before you know it. Also, be ready to sit down and foot your way through if you do lose your balance. In enduros the important thing is to keep going and get through the obstacle, expending the least amount of energy possible, rather than worrying about style and keeping your feet up—leave that to the trials riders! (*Adam Duckworth*)

74

be pulled around as the bike skids, making balance extremely difficult. With your elbows up and bent and your head over the bike's pivot point, then any sudden tugs on the bars can be absorbed better by your arms, without moving too much of your body, thus making it easier to control your machine.

Look out for any branches that are poking out and up towards you, especially the ones at radiator height (if your bike is watercooled, that is). They are the ones that can bang a hole in a radiator, or just as easily jam in your wheel and send you flying over the bars. Sometimes there are logs underneath all the branches and these will not move when you hit them. They will have you off. Also keep a very wary eye out for stumps. Often, the course goes up where a fire break has been cleared in a forest. Not all the tree stumps will be covered and they need to be avoided as they not only cause punctures but can pitch you off with consummate ease.

Where branches are at varying angles across the course, for instance, where forestry vehicles have made a track, then you will have to take it very steadily and try to pick your way through as carefully as possible. These types of tracks are completely unpredictable and your efficient passage through the obstacle will be down to luck as much as to skilful balance and throttle control. When you hit a branch at the wrong angle, it will pitch you off, no matter who you are.

3   Rocky climbs

A rock-scattered climb is one of the trickiest hazards you can encounter on an enduro bike as rocks can be real momentum killers. Obviously they can come in many shapes and sizes, but broadly speaking they break down into two types—loose rocks, and the bigger ones which are generally embedded in the ground.

As with any climb, gaining the initial momentum is very important in order to get you to the top. The main difference, if there are rocks however, is that you will have to read the terrain ahead of you in greater detail than usual to 'plan' your route, section by section, while also looking as far ahead as you can, again to help with selecting your route. The way to get up a rock-covered climb is not to charge at it, as you might for a normal hill, but to approach it with a lot more thought and care.

You should be trying to ride up in second or third gear, depending obviously on the climb itself, laying off the clutch completely, and picking your way up by steering around the worst rocks and using whatever torque your engine has. Don't pick the shortest line up the climb, pin the throttle, and hope for the best. Some of the large rocks can be jumped, using the same technique as that detailed in the chapter on jumping uphill but only where it suits your strategy for the whole climb.

You will be able to exercise better control over the bike in a standing position where all of your body can help with balance and weight distribution than if you are sitting down. If the climb allows, however, you should try to sit down and get more power on, ready to get back into the standing position when the going gets tricky again. If you get knocked off balance and have to sit down and start using your legs to keep going, it is often advisable to stay seated and keep going, using your legs, rather than trying to get to your feet again as quickly as possible. Function always scores over style in enduros and you must always try to keep that momentum going at all costs.

4 Bogs

Like most obstacles you come across during an enduro, bogs vary in size and density. By that I don't mean just their viscosity. Some areas can be strewn with them—big, small, wide and narrow, but all of them have one thing in common—they're all deep! Sometimes you come across a huge one sitting there all on its own, waiting for you... But big or small, the technique needed to cross a bog is broadly similar for all of them, although you will need to assess each on its own merits before launching yourself gung-ho at it.

Let's take the worst scenario first, the big and very deep, rutted bog. You know the one... It's lying there, smiling at you, surrounded by marker arrows directing you straight through the middle of its black, watery mouth, thinly disguised with tall, reed grass. You may also recognize it instantly as one of the bottomless, bike-swallowing varieties. Sometimes the quickest, least painful and least tiring method to get over it, is the same as the technique for bad ditches. Get off the bike and, running alongside it, give it plenty of throttle, fire the clutch and sling it over to the other side. Then swim over or walk round to the other side, pick up your fallen steed, fire it up and carry on. Not very high tech, I know, but effective!

If you decide it is rideable though, approach it with commitment and at a reasonable speed. Loft the front wheel just before the edge of the bog using a combination of throttle and clutch and try to wheelie through, leaving your back wheel to hit the water of the far side of the bog. The very last thing you want to happen is for the front wheel to come down too early, namely, in the middle of the bog. If it does, you'll be in for a quick and ultimately wet trip over the handlebars! The larger the bog, the higher you want your front wheel.

Obviously, once your rear wheel collects the water or the soft part of the bog you will run out of traction and your front wheel will drop. The higher you can get your front wheel, the further it will reach across the bog before it comes down. This can easily make all the difference between your front wheel making it to the far side and safety, or not.

Most other bogs can be ridden through or over. The type that congregates in groups (or gangs...) can usually be ridden through quite easily by reading ahead to avoid the worst ones and any very green grass (which always spells wet ground and potential trouble), and by keeping the front wheel light and just skipping across them.

Careful control of your throttle is vital to maintaining forward motion and traction rather than giving it big fistfulls that might push you off your chosen direction and can easily cause excessive wheel spin. This will only sap your momentum and result in you grinding to a steaming halt in the deepest part of the bog.

Another tip is to take to higher ground where possible. This is not only likely to be drier, but may also present you with another line through the boggy going. Obviously, where markers quite clearly indicate that you have to go straight through a bog, course cutting cannot be condoned and you must give the bog your best shot and try either of the methods described above to get across it.

ABOVE LEFT
Make sure to keep your speed up (and, therefore, momentum) as you approach the bog and shift your weight towards the back of the bike (*Adam Duckworth*)

LEFT
Keep your weight back as you start to lift the front wheel clear of the bog, using a combination of throttle and clutch (*Adam Duckworth*)

ABOVE
The bigger the bog, the higher you want to lift your front wheel, as this will mean it travels further before coming back down to earth. Notice, in this close-up, how Ady has only one finger slipping the clutch so that the rest of his hand is free to hold on to the handlebar (*Adam Duckworth*)

ABOVE LEFT
Ady has judged how high he needs to lift the front wheel in order for it to carry to the far side of this bog (*Adam Duckworth*)

LEFT
The front wheel is starting to come down as the rear wheel nears the centre point of the bog. Notice how the body position is more central than in the approach phase. If your weight is still to the back of the bike at this point, your landing will be more awkward to control (*Adam Duckworth*)

ABOVE
Touchdown on the other side of the bog and he didn't even get his boots wet! Remember to keep the power on as the front wheel comes down, in order to keep up your momentun (*Adam Duckworth*)

5 Ditches

Ditches are a bit like that species of apparently mobile tree which seems to have an unnerving and inexplicable affinity for motorcycles. Have you ever noticed on those occasions when you have been knocked off course towards a clump of trees, how the trees move closer together just when you think you have managed to miss them. Or if you do just clear them, how one of their brethren boldly steps up directly in your path and you find out what happens when fragile *homo sapiens* meets immovable, deep-rooted object? Well, ditches are pretty darn similar — they pop up, or rather disappear down, just where you least want or expect them to.

Ironically enough, most ditches are actually easier the faster they are taken. I remember one ditch (probably a wadi) that opened up beneath me as I was racing in a rally in the Sahara, miles from anywhere. It was probably a good 3–4 m across and about a metre or so deep. I only really saw it when I was airborne across it! Because I had been riding in deep sand, the throttle was wide open, my weight well back and the front end light, otherwise I could have made a very nasty dent in the far wall of the ditch. . .

Most of the ditches you are liable to come across are unlikely to be such bike-eaters and can be cleared relatively easily, provided you see them in time. Whenever you are riding in the rough, off-road, you should be scanning ahead of you all the time, looking out for obstacles like ditches. Once you spot one, there are a variety of techniques you can use to hop across it, depending on the size of the ditch and your speed.

You should aim to loft the front wheel so that it clears the entire ditch and then bunny-hop the rear of the bike over too, or simply let the rear wheel hit the far side of the ditch and your rear suspension take care of the impact. At lower speeds you should approach the ditch in the standing attack position, push down with your arms to pre-load your front suspension just before the lip, and then accelerate as it recoils, launching the front end clear of the ditch and leaving the back end to take care of the hit.

Alternatively, if you are going a bit quicker, rather than loading up the front, use your throttle and clutch together to get the front end up. Then, using your legs like springs, pre-load the rear suspension to bunny-hop over to the other side; gripping the bike with your legs will help you get the back of the bike in the air. Until you have perfected bunny-hopping, concentrate on getting the front end up and over by using the throttle and your clutch and simply let the back end hit the far side. Your rear suspension should have no trouble coping with the hits but make sure you are ready and keep your weight in the middle of the bike to avoid being thrown forward due to the rear wheel's impact.

If you think the ditch is too big and ugly to risk jumping, then the safest thing to do is to get off the bike, run alongside it while it is in gear, fire the clutch and throttle as you get to the edge, launch the bike across to the other side and just let go. Be careful if you do adopt this 'technique' to give it the same commitment as you would if you were on the bike. The last thing you want is to let it go half-cocked and end up with the bike sitting on its side in the middle of the ditch, while you look on, red-faced from the side.

ABOVE RIGHT
With this type of ditch or gully (as opposed to the ditches found on flatter ground), the approach is all-important. You should take your time on the downslope, but move towards the water with enough speed to set you up for the climb out on the other side (*Adam Duckworth*)

RIGHT
Start to move your body forwards into a more upright riding position, keeping you arms slightly bent as you head towards the water, so that you can still steer the bike without moving your body too much. If you keep your arms straight, you can easily be knocked off balance. At this point, you should have assessed what path you want to take to climb out of the gully and will be accelerating to gain momentum (*Adam Duckworth*)

ABOVE
In this example, as Ady climbs out of the gully, he is preparing to tackle a small ledge directly ahead of him and is using a combination of body positioning and throttle to maintain grip (*Adam Duckworth*)

ABOVE RIGHT
The rear wheel is hidden by the ledge, but the front is clear of the lip and he has enough momentum to clear the obstacle that could otherwise have halted his progress. Ady has straightened his legs to push the back of the bike down to maintain grip as the rear wheel is about to collect the ledge (*Adam Duckworth*)

RIGHT
Both wheels have cleared the ledge, and Ady has his legs flexed again to help his balance near the top of the gully and to maintain that all-important traction at the back wheel (*Adam Duckworth*)

6 Forest roads

For this book, forest roads are defined as gravel roads that twist through and around forests. They are composed of coarse gravel and have no centre ridge (as for instance tracks would) and usually feature steep cambers, particularly on corners. They are a common feature of Welsh enduros, but similar roads can also be found in events all over the British Isles.

One of the main problems with this type of going is that the stones can easily cause punctures. As an aside, everyone has their own methods for preventing punctures. Each has a proven 100 per cent record (supposedly...) and each rider swears that his or hers is the best technique.

Try your own, but a few I have come across are reasonably well accepted. Cut the valve out of an old tube and carefully cut the tube along the inside seam, it can then be placed over your good tube to form a second skin. Inflate the good tube to something approaching the size it would be in your tyre and put insulating tape around the two tubes about every quarter. This will loosely hold the second tube on to the good one when fitting the tyre and won't interfere with the good tube when you are riding.

Many punctures are caused when the tube gets pinched against the sidewall of the tyre and the wheel rim. This 'impact puncture' can happen when the tyre gets flattened under impact with a rock or sharp edge. Liberal use of talcum powder when fitting the tube in the tyre can help to prevent this. Some riders simply pump their tyre pressures up and knowingly sacrifice some grip in order to run their tyres a bit harder than they should to try and combat impact punctures.

A motocross-style riding technique is the safest one to use on forest roads as it offers you the best position to control your bike effectively. Braking should be carried out in a standing position and not in the 'classic' enduro-riding style where the backside appears glued to the saddle!

Get up out of the saddle and you will find your bike easier to control, particularly if it starts to slide or drift. If the entire corner is visible it should be ridden using the same technique as described for flat corners and remember, *keep those elbows up!* Most enduro riders can be spotted a mile away by the position of their elbows while cornering. We have all seen it and all been guilty of it at some time or other. Elbows tucked comfortably into the body, drooping down, is easy on the arms, but is far from conducive to machine control.

If the entire corner is invisible, a more cautious approach should be adopted. Look for any obvious line that may have been carved into the corner. If none is apparent, then simply hug the inside of the corner and let the back end of the bike drift as you see the corner unfolding. Most corners follow the contours of the land to such an extent that you can predict which are likely to tighten up on you, and which are more open.

From my own experience in the Tour of Wales Enduro one year, I remember a long section of forest road that followed the contours of the hills for most of the way and was pretty easy. There was one corner in particular that looked a little tighter than the normal left hander. I set myself up for it in the normal way and braked deep into what I could see of the apex before setting myself up in the seated cornering position, with outside elbow up and leaning the bike into the corner while hugging the inside line.

I was feeling suitably stylish and was still in a good position when the corner started to tighten and I noticed a few lines disappearing over the edge of the far side of the corner where preceding riders had obviously been caught out and locked up before sliding over the edge into the ditch. This didn't cause me a problem and I smiled quietly to myself at their, hopefully harmless, misfortune and carried on around the corner, accelerating a bit harder, expecting to see the end of the corner.

I had laughed too soon. The corner tightened again and this time I joined yet another series of lines heading for the edge as I locked up the back brake. I missed the ditch but took off, heading for a landing amongst some large and very painful looking rocks. Shutting my eyes as I landed, I waited for everything to stop and the pain to tell me where I was hurt! To my surprise, nothing hurt too much and I opened my eyes just as a converted RM 250 Suzuki came around the same corner.

He too followed the same line, slid his bike sideways and joined me amongst the rocks but got a better landing. 'Are you alright?' He said. 'I was using you as a pace setter on this bit. I figured if you got round the corners OK, I would too. I bet that one's had a few people off today!' We shared a laugh before extricating our bikes and carrying on again.

Most of the time you should ride in the centre of the road in the seated attack position and cut in tight on the flatter corners, without getting out of the saddle, and without diving down into the camber to cut the corner. In lots of instances though, another line will have been made in the lee of the camber on a bend and it is perfectly safe to follow this too.

If it is wet, forest roads can be slippery and very treacherous and it is worth reminding yourself that the enduro is a timed trial and not a flat-out race. Finishing at the next the check on time is what matters and not going as fast as you can.

7 In and around trees

It is always easier to ride around trees than to try riding up them. Sounds simple enough doesn't it, but just how many times have we all tried it or seen other people endeavouring to do it?

The trouble begins when the course departs from a nice straight line and starts to twist in and out around the trees. This is when things start to get interesting and a little more complicated and where the good forest riders get sorted out from the rest.

Some riders advocate the technique whereby you hang off the bike in order to keep the bike relatively upright and thus achieve a quicker line through the trees. This doesn't really stand up in practice and should only be used as a last-ditch manoeuvre when a branch or whole tree is about to unseat you.

The best method is to keep with the bike and stay seated where possible. Keep your elbows up to help the steering and purchase for the front tyre. Speed through wooded sections will be achieved by reading ahead, co-ordination, establishing a rhythm and timing, as you flick the bike around the trees. Try to keep as close to each tree as you can without clipping it. Treat them as if they were a series of slalom poles— the only trouble is that unlike in ski racing, these ones aren't spring loaded! If your concentration wanders, then you will start to loose your rhythm and begin to hit the trees.

Over the course of an enduro, especially where there is more than one lap, roots will start to become exposed as riders follow the same line close to the base of the trees. There is no secret to riding over roots. You either stay on when you ride over them, or come off. The choice is rarely yours. One thing you should do if they are really bad is to look for alternative lines. Another line may be to use the base of another tree as a berm and ride off that. In some cases the only thing you can do is to look for a new line altogether, provided you are still able to keep within the course markers.

This type of acute, S-shaped turn shows how important it is to plan a route quickly in order to achieve a smooth passage. Ady has seen the stump immediately ahead of him and has already decided to take the route beside it, rather than over the top (*Adam Duckworth*)

Notice how he is using only one or two fingers, rather than all four, to cover the clutch and front brake as he moves towards the stump. This way he can hang on to the handlebars with the rest of his hand and maintain control (*Adam Duckworth*)

Even though some branches are in his way, Ady leans into them to counter their drag and to keep his balance. He has made sure the front wheel is where he wants it to be as it approaches the lip beside the stump, and is only putting his head down to prevent any chances of it getting caught on the branches (*Adam Duckworth*)

ABOVE
Clear of the branches, Ady is making sure his front wheel misses the root to the right of his wheel as he guides the bike down the slope, past the stump, and prepares to turn to the right (*Adam Duckworth*)

ABOVE
Notice how Ady has shifted his body to the outside of the bike, as both wheels clear the stump and root and he makes the turn to the right before carrying on through the trees (*Adam Duckworth*)

RIGHT
Always approach water crossings with a great deal of caution. Only ride through feet up if you can see the bottom clearly. Otherwise, sit down and use your feet like outriggers (*Adam Duckworth*)

8 River and water crossings

Watercrossings can be good fun and very spectacular, but can also become a major embarrassment very quickly if your bike gets flooded and coughs to a halt, or if you find a slippery rock and drop the bike midstream.

If you can't see the bottom clearly and the water looks possibly very deep, the safest option is to get off and walk the bike across while using the throttle and clutch to trickle the bike along in first gear. That way, if there are any large rocks or strong currents, you can be sure of dragging the bike through, rather than running the risk of slipping off on a slippery rock and tipping the bike into the water, where you could flood the engine and carburettor. Also, by getting off the bike, you are allowing it to sit higher in the water, thus raising your air intake further from the water level than it would otherwise have been with your weight on the bike.

If the crossing looks rideable, you should enter very slowly to avoid splashing too much water near your electrics or the carburettor. Keep a low gear and try to trickle through the water slowly, using very delicate throttle control while keeping your legs extended like outriggers to help you balance. Stay loose and relaxed on the bike rather than hanging on too tightly and gripping the bike with your legs for all you are worth. Only if the crossing is shallow and you can see the bottom clearly, should you try to ride through feet up. Otherwise, if there is the slightest risk of awkward rocks lurking under the surface, do away with worrying about style and keep your feet down, just in case. Better safe than wet. . .

ABOVE LEFT
If your are going to ride through feet up, keep
your elbows up and bent and don't grip the bike
too tightly. Stay relaxed and you will be able to
control the machine more easily
(*Adam Duckworth*)

LEFT
By staying loose on the bike, Ady has been able to
quickly react as the front wheel darts off a small
rock (*Adam Duckworth*)

ABOVE
Crossing successfully accomplished, and the bike
continues to scurry over the rocks as a nasty,
rocky climb unfolds ahead. You can see how
flexible and loose you have to stay on the bike by
comparing the body positions Ady has had to use
to negotiate this crossing (*Adam Duckworth*)

9 Off cambers

Off-camber turns are commonly found in enduros, particularly on hillsides and are one of the most genuinely taxing tests of a rider's technique and skill. Approach is once again, all important.

Look ahead as you are coming down the hill towards the off-camber section. If you are turning left, your head should be looking left, checking for any roots under trees, rocks, or anything else which could upset your momentum. Body positioning is essential to riding off cambers successfully. You should be in a standing position with your weight over the back of the bike. The bike should be leant into the camber and therefore slightly away from the hill, while your body is leant into the hill and away from the camber. In that way, if the bike does happen to topple over, it won't topple on to you. Never, ever fall on the down side of a camber. If the point of no return has been reached, always try to fall into the hill.

Delicate, controlled braking is very important. Use both the front and rear brakes, feeling your way down with the front brake, so that the bike isn't sliding all over the place, and keep your weight right over the back of the bike. As the camber straightens out, apply delicate throttle control and keep the outside footrest weighted to help keep your grip on the hill.

When preparing for the corner going uphill, you must keep your head up to look ahead and see if there are any natural advantages or lines to help the crucial transition from the off-camber straight to the uphill. Look out for anywhere that you might get stuck. Your body should be at the back of the bike, with your rear hanging off the edge so that your centre of gravity is as far to the outside of the bike as possible.

Aim for a smooth drive out of the camber and find grip by using controlled and sensitive throttle control, without stabbing at your clutch. If the bike is sliding or there is a rut, then you should sit down to execute the turn. If there is very little purchase then you will have more control by standing on the pegs in order to find grip. If you are sitting down, with the power on, the back wheel will be likely to spin and if there is no rut or any dry stuff, then it will slide.

By standing, you can move your body around to try to find grip and control the back wheel. This is where your drive obviously comes from and you have to make sure it is not spinning. As soon as you feel the engine bog or the back wheel start to spin, you need to hit the throttle without causing too much wheelspin. By shifting your weight back, you will help to compensate for the throttle by making the back wheel drive and hopefully find the necessary grip and traction to keep you going. All very easy to describe, but quite tricky to master.

The following sequence illustrates a route coming out of a section of trees and on to a forest road before climbing up an embankment and back into some woods. The weight is over the front as the bike comes up on to the road and the rider sees the embankment ahead of him for the first time (*Adam Duckworth*)

10 Embankments

It used to be quite common practice for a route to put riders into a forest section by making them ride up the face of an embankment to get in among the trees. Nowadays it is more likely that the entry into the forest will be a great deal easier, and up logs or a more defined track.

However, it is still very common to have to drop out of a forest section down an embankment and back on to a forest road. These can be very tricky as the road is normally built up from quite a steep camber, with a big dip where it meets the embankment. Quite often a rut can form at the bottom where everyone before you has come out of the embankment and down on to the road and you have no choice but to

ride down it as you would a normal downhill.

Approach the top of the embankment standing on the pegs and have a quick look over the lip, to see what it is like and what your options are. Then ride down, again standing, until you hit the bottom by the road. If it is a steep drop (and they usually are), then there will be quite a jolt as you sit down in the bottom of the dip. All you can do is to try to lean back a little, to stop being thrown forward and to help cope with the hit, while being ready to use your legs to help paddle you out of any rut that might have formed. If there is room, however, you might find you are better off using a different line and cutting across the slope to give you a smoother ride to the bottom and the road.

TOP
A choice of techniques can be employed here. One is to keep both wheels on the ground and try to simply ride up the embankment. Alternatively, the rider can elect to loft the front wheel, as Ady is about to do here, raising the front by a combination of throttle and clutch and by shifting his weight back slightly (*Adam Duckworth*)

ABOVE
His legs are straightened as he fires the front wheel at the bank (*Adam Duckworth*)

ABOVE RIGHT
The rear wheel collects the base of the bank as the front is about to hit the bank (*Adam Duckworth*)

RIGHT
The momentum has carried the bike half-way up the embankment already and Ady adopts a more central position on the bike, with his knees bent to help control the bike as he continues the rest of the climb (*Adam Duckworth*)

ABOVE
His weight is shifted towards the back while
applying smooth throttle, to maintain traction at
the rear, until the bank starts to level out (*Adam
Duckworth*)

ABOVE
If a route takes you up an embankment and into a forest, it is bound to drop you out at some stage or other. Brake as you come up to the edge of the embankment, feeling your way with both brakes and using just two fingers on the front brake and clutch. Assess the slope before you commit yourself (*Adam Duckworth*)

ABOVE
In this instance, the drop is at an angle to the slope, so the run-off at the bottom should be quite smooth (*Adam Duckworth*)

ABOVE
Keep your weight over the back of the bike as you near the bottom of the bank and the camber of the forest road (*Adam Duckworth*)

ABOVE
Your weight should come forward as the front wheel reaches the cambered slope of the road. In many cases, particularly where the drop is steeper and straight down, there is quite a jolt as you hit the road. In that case, you are probably better off sitting down just as you make contact, being sure to keep your weight well back, otherwise you can easily be thrown forward into (or over) the handlebars (*Adam Duckworth*)

ABOVE
Bring your weight forward as the back wheel
collects the camber and you accelerate out on to
the road (*Adam Duckworth*)

11 Uphills

Gnarly or slippery uphills are one of the most common hazards and give rise to problems for a large number of riders where technique and skilful throttle control are the essentials for a successful climb.

The important part of tackling an uphill is the approach. The faster and smoother the approach, the better it is for you. If you have limited space and a slow, rough approach, things are going to be very difficult. Getting to the top is all about momentum, commitment and aggression on the approach.

Get as much power on at the bottom as possible by using either the standing or seated attack position with your head over the steering head and elbows up, so that the upper part of your body is flexible and the bike can move around without moving your body too much. Get as much speed up as you can to the bottom of the hill itself and keep a seated attack position where possible, ready to shift your weight back down the saddle if needed to find grip. If you can keep a constant speed up the slope, then clutch and throttle should be plenty to get you to the summit.

If, however, you do start to run into difficulty and your speed drops to the extent where you have nearly come to a standstill, you should knock the bike down to as low a gear as possible and endeavour to 'trials ride' the bike up the rest of the hill, trying to leave the clutch alone and relying on delicate throttle control. Sometimes you will find more grip by rolling the power off to create torque rather than, if you are in trouble, pinning it and clutching the bike, which may cause wheelspin and a subsequent halt to your progress. On some hills it will help, where you need the speed rather than the ability to go slow to find grip.

Consider the hill as a complete obstacle, rather than breaking it down into little sections, and try to judge the momentum, speed and revs needed to pull you all the way to the top with ease and without screaming the bike. In that way you should have a little bit in reserve and will be gradually rolling the power off to maintain traction as you get nearer the top.

If you do run into difficulty, then you will need to start to use the techniques described above. The quicker you react, the more chance you will have of keeping your momentum going, even if you have to go at less of a tangent to the hill to get your speed up again. The essential thing is to keep moving ever upwards, even if you have to ride around most of the hill to do it. This is better than grinding to a halt halfway up the hill.

Remember, hill climbing has a great deal to do with commitment at the bottom of the hill and skilful throttle control from then on. As with most skills, this will require lots and lots of practice and experimentation. Go for it!

ABOVE RIGHT
Riding uphill successfully is all about commitment and aggression at the bottom of the hill. Approach under power, in the standing or seated attack position, while planning how much momentum you will need to reach the top of the hill (*Adam Duckworth*)

RIGHT
Keep your elbows up and bent as you make contact with the base of the hill and keep the power on (*Adam Duckworth*)

ABOVE LEFT
If possible, stay seated, keep your elbows up and your weight towards the back of the bike, ready to move to the standing position if necessary. A standing position will make it easier to cope with undulations in the hill (*Adam Duckworth*)

LEFT
Shift your weight to the back if you need to find grip, but be ready to come forward again to prevent looping out! (*Adam Duckworth*)

ABOVE
You will need to be ready to bring your weight forwards over the front of the bike to keep it down as you reach a particularly steep part or the top. Unfortunately, what cannot be illustrated in pictures, or described in words, is the throttle control and riding skill that lets the top riders blast up a hill that will cause many other riders to flounder (*Adam Duckworth*)

12 Downhills

You should *always* approach the lip of a downhill with great caution. If it happens to occur on a special test, you will have had a chance to walk the course, so you should know what the drop is like. On a normal section, however, you won't know what's on the other side. There could be a sheer drop, a bend, roots, rocks, a slight slope or any other permutation of potential hazards, you just don't know so you must exercise caution.

Approach the top of the hill in a standing position following on from your braking position with two fingers only on the front brake, two fingers covering the clutch lever, and your foot on the back brake— ready to stop if it looks nasty or to go if it all looks good. Quickly survey the slope as you are on the lip before committing yourself. You should look for trees, any awkward roots, whether the slope is clear or bracken-covered, where stumps or rocks might be lurking and anything else that you can gain from a quick scan to help you make a safe descent. It's unusual to find any really crazy descents in modern enduros, but you still need that split second to check the slope before you commit yourself.

Some of the trickiest descents are between trees where nine times out of ten there are old tree stumps hidden, waiting to catch you out. Once you have decided to go, ride down in the gear suitable to the prevailing conditions and steepness of the slope, in the standing position with two fingers on the front brake, using whatever amount of pressure suits the hill.

Feel the rear brake only occasionally for control or if you start to go a bit too fast, keep your head up and looking where you are going, and keep your weight over the back wheel. It is also important to keep your elbows up and bent as much as possible while descending, particularly over choppy ground, in order to help control your steering. In most cases you are better off adopting this attack-type position rather than concentrating wholly on getting your weight as far back as possible, which will force you to keep your arms straighter and make any jolts more difficult to control.

Most downhills look worse than they actually are and you will be surprised at the relative ease with which the really steep ones can be tackled, provided you approach them in the right way and with a positive attitude.

ABOVE RIGHT
Approach the top of a hill with caution and in a standing position so that you don't commit yourself until you have had a quick scan of what lies ahead (*Adam Duckworth*)

RIGHT
Get your weight well back as the front drops over the lip of the hill. Make sure you keep your elbows up and slightly bent, even though your weight is so far back. Straight arms on a downhill are bad news (*Adam Duckworth*)

TOP
Stay flexible as you go down the hill. In this case, there is a ridge half-way down and you would need to stab at the clutch and add some throttle in order to lift the front wheel clear of the ridge (*Adam Duckworth*)

ABOVE
The front has cleared the ridge and is kept out of harm's way as the back of the bike is about to impact the bottom of the ridge. The rider's body should always stay relaxed on the bike; keeping those arms up has the additional benefit of forcing your body into the correct position for 'downhilling' (*Adam Duckworth*)

TOP
The rider's weight is brought forwards slightly for the impact into the attack position, as the rear wheel collects the ledge without causing the rider any trouble (*Adam Duckworth*)

ABOVE
You should adopt the attack position as the bottom is reached, making sure to keep your elbows up and bent so that they can absorb any jolt or impact (*Adam Duckworth*)

13　Ruts

Ruts can be the pain of an enduro if they are long and root-ridden, but many simply build up where the choice of routes is limited and where riders have had to follow the same path. They occur in all shapes and sizes and can be found on straights or may build up to something of a berm on long corners.

Many riders find ruts intimidating but the shorter ones that are free of roots or rocks are best taken under power, at a reasonable speed, and with a good deal of commitment. Stand in the attack position but with your weight slightly to the back of the bike.

Try not to think of it as a rut that limits your control of the front wheel but more as a need to ride, steering from the back of the bike, along a given line, namely the exact path of the rut. Stay relaxed on the bike but be ready, if need be, to shift your weight by applying more pressure on either footrest to alter your balance.

If it is a really deep rut then you are better off sitting down and legging your way through it. Keep the front wheel light in case you come to a hole, keep the power on and don't worry about style. Maintain your legs trailing to help you foot through where necessary and just try to keep your momentum going. Some riders prefer to waggle the bars in the rut to counteract any natural overreaction they might have to any sliding or drifting motion. The best method though is to stay relaxed on the bike, keep the front end light and apply steady, controlled throttle. Gently steer into any slides or drifts as they develop, rather than fighting the bike, which can become very tiring over a full day's riding.

As stated earlier, ruts come in a variety of guises. The big, deep, wet ones have got to be tackled gently otherwise you run the risk of getting water in the carburettor, whereas shorter ones can be cleared with the minimal amount of splash by lofting the front over any water using the throttle and clutch, just as you would with small bogs.

Many ruts are caused by four-wheel drive or farm vehicles (or army tanks, as in the popular enduros in Hampshire). Some of these ruts are wide enough to let you ride in them with no trouble at all. Problems can occur even in these wide ruts, however, when hundreds of bikes have gone over the same rut making it deep. In that situation, you are possibly better off climbing out of the rut before the worst patches and riding on the centre strip between the tracks. You can always hop back into the rut if the centre strip has rocks or other obstacles and then climb out of the rut again if it gets too bad—always keep your momentum going.

In these deeper ruts a useful safety tip is to make sure your feet are pointing inwards towards the bike and the balls of your feet are on the rests. This should stop your feet getting caught on the side of the rut and being wrenched backwards and off the footrests. Ady Smith unfortunately learnt this the hard way in one particular enduro and ended up with a broken ankle. Thanks for the tip, Ady.

Some of the most tiring ruts to ride are the ones that build up between trees where the roots become exposed. Momentum is the most important part of riding these successfully. You will almost certainly need to leg your way through them keeping your legs out like stabilisers. Try to use the minimal throttle to help traction, and use your body positioning to push the bike over the worst roots. It can often be worthwhile looking ahead before you get into the worst of the roots to see if you can plan a good route rather than just following the ruts in front of you. Sometimes it pays to get out of a series of ruts by riding at right angles across them in order to find an alternative route. Style is unimportant in the trickiest ruts, getting through them is what counts and keeping that momentum going!

RIGHT
The natural tendency in ruts is to fight the bike and try to make it steer where you want it to. Concentrate on the direction the rut takes, ride it steadily and adjust your weight quickly, but smoothly. Here, Ady is counterbalancing to the left of the bike as the rut turns to the left (*Adam Duckworth*)

FAR RIGHT
A minor correction is needed to keep his balance. . . (*Adam Duckworth*)

110

ABOVE

...and Ady is back in the middle of the bike and ready for anything as the rut straightens out again (*Adam Duckworth*)

ABOVE

It is often necessary to climb out of a rut, and many riders lose their front wheel when they try to ride out. Lean away from the direction you turn the bike (as you would for an off-camber) and apply delicate clutch and throttle control to push the front wheel out of the rut (*Adam Duckworth*)

ABOVE
As the front clears the rut, keep your weight
leaning away from the bike, your elbows up and,
again, through careful use of the clutch and
throttle, gently ride the bike out of the rut. Too
much throttle and haste will only cause the tyre to
lose traction and spin (*Adam Duckworth*)

14 Reading the terrain

There are still a few one-lap enduros left, particularly in Wales, which can offer the rider some large sections of open moorland, with only occasional markers. This puts a lot of onus on the individual rider to read the terrain ahead in order to get from marker to marker as efficiently and quickly as possible. This calls for a quick assessment of the likely route, with a good idea of the broad direction required and allowing for deviations en route, depending on specific obstacles encountered.

Sometimes the markers offer a fairly narrow route already, leaving you to spot any nasty bits and avoid them while staying within the markers. If the markers are quite far apart then you need to look even further ahead. Search for high ground where possible and see if you can find the best way to the next marker.

Areas of bright green grass should always be avoided as well as any bogs you can spot and legitimately miss out. Among the problems of riding at any decent speed over open ground, for example, moorland, are deep, soft patches that stop your front wheel dead and chuck you off over the handlebars if you are not ready for them. As soon as you see them coming up, get your weight back and keep the front end light to stop the front wheel disappearing. Try to judge whether a soft patch is safe to blast through, or whether you would be better off trying to walk the bike through, or taking it at a better angle than simply head-on.

If the route follows the side of a valley or hill and you are not quite sure where the route goes further along, you should normally stay high on the side of the hill until you see the way again. It is always easier to ride vertically down to rejoin a track below you than to try to climb up out of a dip or a series of sheep trails.

Look out for clumps of spectators, especially if they appear to have walked quite a way to reach their vantage points. This always spells potential trouble up ahead. They are sure to be there for a reason and it is unlikely to be to help pull you out of a hole or cheer you on! It probably indicates a particularly big bog, a greasy hill climb, or some other hazard that is best approached with caution.

Reading the terrain is mainly about applying common sense to what is unfolding in front of you. It is not easy to have a good look around when you are busy dealing with the going immediately ahead of you but try to make a point of continually glancing up and having a quick scan for anything that will help you plan your way.

PART THREE

PREPARATION

1 Kitting yourself out properly

Whether you are involved in motocross or enduro you must be properly prepared to enjoy your particular sport to the full and above all, safely. The first thing to attend to is the rider.

Riding motorcycles off-road, you are going to fall off at some stage or other, and you need to wear adequate protective equipment at all times to reduce the chances of injury. The same equipment should be worn whether you are practising or competing for real. Every crash is accidental or unintended. As with all accidents, you can't tell when they are going to happen, so you have to be prepared every time you ride your bike.

Working from the top downwards, you should wear a securely fastened crash helmet that bears either a gold or silver ACU standard. The choice of helmets available to the off-road rider is vast. The single most important factor in buying a helmet is to make sure it fits your head properly. It should be a good, snug fit without any lateral movement.

Most helmet linings will 'give' a little with time and wearing, but if you do experience any discomfort or throbbing in the head after just a few minutes of wearing, then the helmet is probably too small or simply the wrong shape for your head. Try another size, or different helmet. Everyone's head is a different shape and you should try as many different helmets on as possible before narrowing down your selection.

Once you do have a few to choose from that fit you correctly, then pick the best one you can afford. The market is so diverse that it is impossible to recommend brands but as a general rule, the better the quality of the helmet, the more expensive it is likely to be. Your motorcycle club could be a useful source of advice here, but bear in mind that everyone has their own favourite makes and this may colour their impartiality and objectivity.

A crash helmet is an expensive item that should give you at least two to three years service, depending of course on the treatment it receives, so it is worth taking your time over its selection. As the fashion for customizing helmets spreads to the off-road world, it is worth making the point that you should pay special attention to any manufacturer's warnings regarding things such as solvents, paints and stickers. Look after your helmet properly and it will look after you.

There has always been a great deal of debate on the pros and cons of full-face helmets versus open-face types. Some research suggests that the full-face type can cause neck injury in certain circumstances, while the inadequacies of an open-face helmet are obvious if a rider is unlucky enough to land on his or her face.

It would be wrong of me to use this space to voice my own preference because that is all it would be, a preference. There is inadequate research or statistically valid data currently available to judge either way. What has been my experience though, from a wide range of uses off-road, is that both types have disadvantages in varying circumstances, but that you are undoubtedly far better off wearing one or other than nothing at all.

If you do decide on an open-face helmet, then it is advisable to wear a face guard such as the Scott face protector featured in the picture, or something similar, depending on the brand of goggle you choose to wear. This will offer only limited protection in the event of a fall, face first, but will deflect stones, mud, branches, etc.

This brings me quite neatly to goggles. In 1987 the government decreed that all eye protection should carry the British Standard kitemark, although a particular quirk of the law is that it is not compulsory to wear eye protection, neither need it be in good condition. However, goggles should be worn at all times and lenses replaced if they become too scratched.

Some riders find goggles a trifle inhibiting and complain of restricted vision and misting problems. However, it is worth persevering with them and getting used to wearing them all the time. Any slight restriction of vision is more than made up for by the benefits in terms of eye protection.

Ready to ride, be it motocross or enduro. The protective gear being worn underneath the shirt and pants is barely noticeable, but the rider is protected by body armour, kidney belt, hip protectors and knee/shin protectors (*Vic Barnes*)

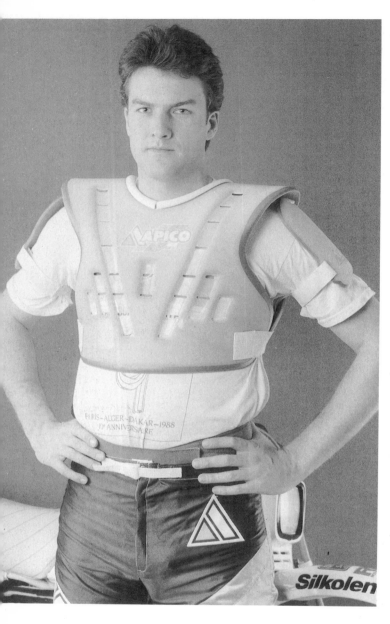

Front view of good quality body armour, showing the amount of ventilation and arm mobility designed for comfort, and the padding that provides protection for the chest, collar bone and shoulder areas (*Vic Barnes*)

Body armour, or body protectors, can normally be worn either under or over a shirt. Technology and designs are changing all the time, and you should find something that feels comfortable to wear. Other riders are a useful source of information as to which types are uncomfortable or may restrict movement. The important thing is to make sure you wear some sort of body protector as, once again, anything is better than nothing at all, even for enduro riders. It is important to find something that offers back protection, too, rather than just chest protection.

Back protectors come in a variety of types; the most common is the 'kidney belt'. As its name implies, this provides support and protection for the kidney area. Judging by the way some riders wear them, they are not too sure just where their kidneys are. If they injure them they certainly will! Many kidney belts are worn too high on the abdomen. The kidneys are in the lower back, not under the ribs, which is where a lot of belts appear to be worn by riders, like some sort of male bra! Most modern kidney belts also incorporate some degree of lower spine protection. They should be worn at all times.

Most off-road riding pants or trousers come with detachable hip protectors, normally held in place by Velcro, or something similar. Make sure these are worn the right way round so that they protect the whole hip area and not just the joint.

Among the most vulnerable parts of the body, in the event of coming off, are the knees. Some pants are designed to incorporate a knee cup, but most knee protectors are separate and have a flexible joint connecting the knee cup to a shin protector. These can be fixed in position by a variety of methods, including a separate lining in the trouser leg. I have found the most effective at staying in position are the type that have a single, elasticated strap that goes behind the calf muscle. Once again, there are many types, and it is important to wear something rather than ride without any knee protection at all.

The items of protective gear that most riders view with nostalgia and wax lyrical about are their riding boots, recounting endless tales of how long they lasted and how many times they saved their legs from serious injury. Whichever brand you choose, make sure that they are comfortable and can be made to fit snugly around your lower leg by a draw-string and either buckles or some other fastening. As high fashion takes over the off-road riding apparel market, excellent value in boots can always be found if your prerequisites are for quality of construction rather than the very latest design. The boots you eventually choose should ideally have reinforced soles, be made of a good quality leather and offer reasonable shin and ankle protection.

If you are prone to an occasional cynical tendency, you might make the easy mistake of thinking that motocross pants, or jeans as they are otherwise known, were designed primarily to advertise the pants' brand name, rather than provide any practical function such as making motorcycle riding more comfortable. In spite of the ever increasing space and size given to the brand name, there are some good motocross jeans out there, as well as some average quality ones. The main thing to look at is the quality of the material. Even up to quite recently, the only material to be seen in was leather, while some manufacturers produced pants made out of a material very similar to denim.

Nowadays, most pants are made out of nylon-based materials. The plain nylon trousers are generally cheaper but wear out quicker. The better quality motocross jeans use a satin nylon material with a wax treatment on one side. This not only makes the trousers softer and more comfortable to wear, but is also tougher than plain nylon.

Most pants also feature a synthetic, leather-like knee patch for the side of the knee and calf. This makes gripping the bike with the legs easier and more comfortable. The synthetic nature of the materials in modern pants means that a wider variety of colours and designs can be employed and that they can be easily machine washed without detriment to the appearance and durability of the trouser.

Certain brands have built-in protective, padded areas for the upper thigh and hip area; in some cases these are cleverly blended in with the overall design so that you can benefit from additional protection without sacrificing any of that all important track-style credibility!

A good quality riding shirt is needed to top off and complete the attire for motocross, and the variety of these supercedes that for any other item of equipment. Enduro riders will prefer to have something a bit more substantial and there are a number of good enduro jackets on the market. Most of these incorporate a number of useful features, such as adjustable vents along the back which can be opened when the going gets hot, and closed when the section opens out and gets colder again. Prices vary a great deal, but so does the quality. Again, satin nylon is good and can be easily washed clean. Otherwise,

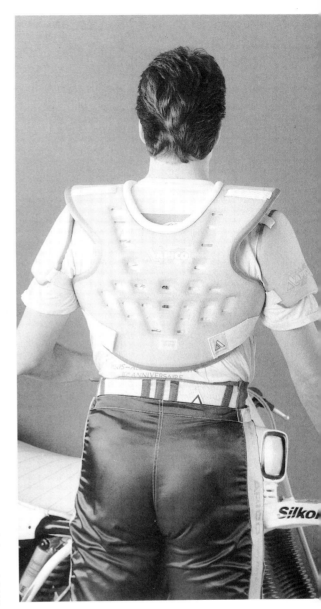

Rear view of the same body armour, the level of back protection being evident, as well as the adjustable shoulder protectors. The kidney belt, plus its reinforcements for lower spine protection, are seen here being worn in the correct position. Only the top half of the belt is visible above the riding pants (*Vic Barnes*)

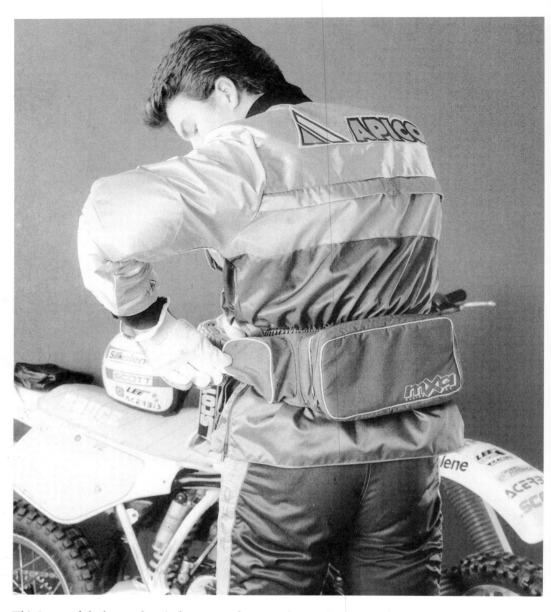

This is one of the best enduro jackets currently available on the market, being tough and waterproof, while bristling with useful features that any enduro rider will appreciate. These include the compartment in the elbow that contains an elbow protector, vents that can be opened or closed along the back of the shoulders, and adjustable side flaps. The tool belt featured here is used by many top riders and, apart from having the space to hold a spare inner tube and as many tools and parts as you would want to carry, is relatively unobtrusive to wear while riding, is extremely strong and will last for ages (*Vic Barnes*)

If you prefer to use an open-face helmet, it is
advisable to wear it in conjunction with a face
protector, such as the SCOTT model featured
here. The design of face masks has evolved over a
number of years into an accessory that is quite
comfortable to wear, while serving to ward off
stones and branches without causing goggles
to mist up (*Vic Barnes*)

have a look at the more traditional, waxed cotton type of jacket.

Finally, you need to look after your hands. The better quality motocross gloves are exactly what you will need for enduro riding too. You should look for a glove with a soft, pliant palm, but with padding of some sort on the tops of the hand and fingers. Gloves need to fit very well, otherwise they can bunch up when your hands get hot and make operating the controls a little awkward.

A useful tip to prevent blisters on the hands and feet, if you haven't ridden for a while or only ride occasionally, is the liberal application of talcum powder in the gloves and boots before you go out to ride. This works because the talc absorbs some of the sweat, keeping the skin dry.

As with all forms of motor sport, riding a motorcycle off-road can be potentially dangerous. Do not underestimate the need to be prepared for the worst. Wear the best protective riding equipment you can afford and wear it all the time. Safe riding!

2 Looking after your bike

Entire books have been written on this subject and extremely competent race mechanics have taken this aspect of 'preparation' a long way from the traditional spanner-wielding, servicing routines into something almost approaching a science. All I will attempt to do here is to pass on a few tips from the top, and to suggest where you can find the advice and information needed to keep your machine in good running order.

It is essential to run a new bike in properly before trying to get the maximum out of it in competition conditions. Even some suspension needs up to six hours of running in before it will work efficiently. Before going out on your new pride and joy you ought to check over every nut and bolt on the bike, and then only when you have done this, go out and just ride the machine. As with any new engine, take it steady at first and don't over-rev it or make the engine labour in too low a gear. Run a full tank of fuel through—being sure to use a running-in mixture (refer to your manual for the exact ratio) if it's a two-stroke—before you start to explore the engine's capabilities. It's also worth stopping at frequent intervals to check if your spokes need tightening.

Once you have completed running in, a useful tip is to check the oil filter and gearbox oil for any signs of swarf or other metal fragments which might indicate a potential problem. Clean the bike, and then take it apart! This is the only way to check it fully. Pull the suspension bearings apart and grease them with a high quality, saltwater-proof grease. This will not only lubricate the bearings but will also keep them waterproofed.

Check that the wheel bearings are clean and give them similar treatment to the suspension bearings. The bearing surface of the brake caliper on a disc brake is often neglected and a high temperature lubricant should be used here. The two most neglected bearings are the steering head and swinging-arm (or pivoted-fork) bearings. Water tends to seep down into the bottom bearing of the steering head from cleaning, and swinging arms get packed with mud.

A bike should be prepared prior to cleaning, especially if you are going to use a high pressure hose, as neglect in this area can lead to damaged bearing seals as well as many other problems. Be sure to cover the end of the exhaust with a plastic bag, sealed with an elastic band, or a waterproof bung of some sort. Sealing the airbox is also crucial if your bike is not to become water cooled in places it shouldn't. Sometimes the bike can be simply wiped clean rather than turning the hose on to it.

The procedure after cleaning is just as important as the preparation before cleaning. Contact cleaner can be used on the cables and all bearings should be greased both to lubricate during cleaning and to waterproof afterwards.

A point worth bearing in mind is chain adjustment. The point at which the chain is going to be at its maximum tension is when the gearbox sprocket is in a straight line with the swinging-arm pivot and the rear-wheel spindle. This is the best position to have the bike in when checking for the correct tension. Experience will teach you quite quickly to feel for the correct amount of tension. This will be about $1-1\frac{1}{2}$ in. (or 2.5–4.0 cm). A quick check for proper alignment is to look down the chain from the rear sprocket to the front sprocket. If the chain follows a perfectly straight path, then the two sprockets will be in line.

Some new bikes come complete with at least a full workshop manual and there are also race preparation manuals too. These are essential reading if you intend to do all the work yourself and are a handy point of reference for the experts as well. They can all normally be obtained from the importers or their appointed dealers.

Other than the few tips mentioned above, the best advice for bike preparation is to get the workshop and race preparation manuals. Many of the jobs are quite straightforward and can easily be carried by most people without the need for any special tools. But if you are uncertain about maintenance or don't have the proper facilities, then go to the experts rather than trying to do the job yourself. For your bike to operate as it was designed to and to keep it running safely, it needs to be maintained properly and half measures won't do. If in doubt, seek advice.

3   Finding out about the sport

Motocross and enduro events are organized in Britain by two groups, the Auto Cycle Union (ACU) and the Amateur Motorcycle Association (AMCA). The ACU is recognized internationally and is a member of the Federation Internationale Motocycliste (FIM). It has nearly 800 affiliated clubs which are spread throughout the country in 20 centres, according to the area, with a membership of roughly 60,000 split between all aspects of motorcycle sport.

An exciting development in 1988 was the announcement of sponsorship by the National Westminster Bank for an Off-Road Training Scheme, in conjunction with the ACU and under the banner of the Natwest Bank/ACU Training Division. This will involve the setting up of training centres all over Britain where riders can simply practise or make use of ACU-approved instructors, who will teach the riders in a controlled environment and on a specially built site.

The jewel in the crown of this new initiative is The National Motocross and Trials Park at Worcester run by Tim Matthews. His centre sets an example to others by not just limiting itself to hardened enthusiasts but by throwing its doors open to all sections of the community, including social service projects. This is not only good for the overall image and long-term future of motorcycle sport, but will doubtless introduce new participants to the sport who might otherwise never have had the chance to find out just how much fun dirt bikes can be. The centre at Worcester also runs residential courses as well as group or individual training and its facilities include a supercross track, a motocross practice track, a beginners' oval and a trials section suitable for both beginners and experts.

It is hoped that the Natwest Bank/ACU Training Division will be able to open further centres around the country in the near future and develop this important area of off-road sport.

The AMCA is an independent organization catering largely for the amateur rider. It was created in 1932 and aimed to exclude the 'works riders' who were around then and competed on mainly British thumpers, but with the benefits of special frames and other parts provided by their respective factories. Even now, the emphasis within the AMCA is for riders only being permitted to enter bikes on general sale, in order to make competition more even handed and for riders with a genuine interest in the sport rather than any attractions of prize money.

Another avenue open to riders wishing to benefit from training, are the numerous riding schools organized by various importers and concessionaires. These are generally supervised by established or retired motocross stars and are often open to riders with makes of machine other than just the ones sold by the importer responsible for the particular school.

As mentioned earlier, motorcycle clubs are an excellent way of finding out about off-road sport. They cover the entire country, so there is bound to be one near your home. You can find out just where they meet quite easily by contacting either the ACU or

AMCA whose addresses are listed below.

One of the reasons that training centres like the one at Worcester have opened up, apart from their training facility, is to offer riders a place to practise that is both safe and legal. There are a number of motocross tracks that open up on certain days as practice tracks, but so many riders looking for somewhere to practise or simply ride for fun are forced to use land that may be private or belong to the local council, or have to ride through woodland areas. This is not vandalism. None of these riders intends to cause damage or any trouble. They are simply out to enjoy riding their motorcycles and are left with little choice of place to ride other than the old quarry, bit of wasteground or wherever it is that their mates ride. More training centres and practice tracks are definitely needed to offer people the chance to ride their bikes without getting chased away, and where they can be safe and supervised.

One of the problems facing those trying to find new places to build tracks or training centres, is the pressure on land and the uses it is put to. One of the problems with off-road bikes is their noise. Every rider has a part to play in promoting the image of motorcycling and the first thing we can all do is to make sure that the bike's silencer is in good condition and is as quiet as possible.

Manufacturers have started to recognize their responsibilities too and have made positive efforts to reduce noise output, for which they are to be applauded, but there is still room for improvement and they should try even harder to produce motocross and enduro bikes much quieter than they are at present. High performance engines don't necessarily have to be noisy and if the motorcycle industry doesn't take it upon itself to introduce much lower noise levels, then 'somebody else' undoubtedly will.

Useful addresses

THE NATIONAL MOTOCROSS AND TRIALS
PARK,
off Junction 6, M5 Motorway
Worcester

Telephone: 0905 28022

NATWEST/ACU TRAINING DIVISION,
Miller House
Corporation Street
Rugby, Warwickshire CV21 2DN

Telephone: 0788 540179

AMATEUR MOTOR CYCLE ASSOCIATION
Darlaston Road
Walsall WS2 9XL

Telephone: 0922 39517

LEFT
'You won't put this one in the book will you, Neil?'
Sorry, Roger, I couldn't resist it . . .